Level 1 Student's Book

Multilevel English Grammar Programme

John Shepherd

PHOENIX
ELT

incorporating
PRENTICE HALL MACMILLAN

New York   London   Toronto   Sydney   Tokyo   Singapore

First published 1995 by
Phoenix ELT
A division of Prentice Hall International (UK) Ltd
Campus 400, Spring Way
Maylands Avenue, Hemel Hempstead
Hertfordshire, HP2 7EZ

Typeset in Bembo.
by Microset Graphics Ltd., Basingstoke

Printed and bound in Hong Kong

Library of Congress Cataloging-in-Publication Data

British Library Cataloguing in Publication Data

A catalogue record for this book is available from
the British Library

ISBN 0 13 238726 3
ISBN 0 13 238734 4

5   4   3   2   1
1999   98   97   96   95

INTRODUCTION
TO THE TEACHER

The Series

The English Grammar Programme is published in four books, which correspond approximately to the following levels:

Book 1 Elementary   In the region of 50hrs of learning
Book 2 Lower Intermediate   In the region of 150 hrs of learning
Book 3 Intermediate   In the region of 250 hours of learning
Book 4 Upper Intermediate   In the region of 350 hours of learning
                              (preparing for the First Certificate in English, Cambridge University)

This book can be used for self-study or in the classroom.

You will not need to follow the order of units in the book; you are free to choose the order which suits you and your students.

The items have been divided into sections on different grammatical areas, and at the end of each section there is a unit (or sometimes two units) of review and further practice. These can be used for revision, and to check if students are now confident in their handling of the items.

Learning Grammar

Grammar is central to learning a language. When you learn your own language you learn to use the grammar by "osmosis", so to speak. Whether you are taught formally or not, you learn the grammar.

When you learn a foreign language after the age of puberty, you often learn it formally: you listen, you study the grammar, you read, you write, you learn vocabulary and phrases, and you seek opportunities to use the language.

Any teaching can be made enjoyable; the best learning is through laughter. The grammar of a language must be learnt if you are to know the language, but there are many ways of learning.

In the general introduction in the *Teacher's Book*, we discuss the teaching and learning of grammar in more detail.

The Teacher's Book

The *Teacher's Book* gives you, for each unit:
1   Notes on the presentation
2   Suggestions for handling the exercises
3   Common errors
4   Detailed notes on each grammatical point

In the Introduction, you will find:
1   A Preface for each book
2   A General Introduction on learning grammar
3   Practical Notes on how to use the book, with lots of ideas for the classroom.

Studying Alone

This young woman is studying English grammar alone using this book.

Here is what she is doing:

First, she looks at the presentation:

Study the text, notice the date (the year 1000), and look at these pictures.

At 8 am on June 1st in the year 1000....
Where was the Queen? And where were the princesses?

The Queen was in bed.   *Her daughters were in the garden.*
The King wasn't in bed.

Now she looks at the first exercise:

① Now complete these with the words from the box.

was	were
wasn't	weren't

1   The King..........in the kitchen.
2   ....the boys in the garden? No, they .... .They were on the roof of the palace.
3   Where..............the Queen? She............in the kitchen; she..............in bed.
4   The girls.............in the kitchen; they............in the garden.

Now she looks at the grammar *if she wants to*:

FORM		
Affirmative		
singular	*singular/plural*	*plural*
I was a baby.	**You were** (a child, children).	**We were** boys.
He was a nice boy.		**They were** girls.
She was a lovely girl.		
Interrogative	**Negative**	
Was she a doctor?	**She was not** a nurse.	
Where **were they** yesterday?	**They were not** here last night.	

See also notes for BE in Unit 1

Now she looks at the exercise at the bottom of this page:

Good English?

② Look at the <u>underlined</u> parts of these sentences. Four of them are correct and four are wrong.
Tick (✔) the correct ones, and rewrite the wrong ones.

.... 1   <u>He were</u> in the garden.
.... 2   <u>Was he</u> on the roof?
.... 3   <u>We were</u> in the room.
.... 4   <u>They wasn't</u> in the kitchen.
.... 5   <u>He didn't was</u> there.
.... 6   <u>I was</u> here.
.... 7   <u>Did you were</u> at home?
.... 8   <u>She wasn't</u> in the house.

Now she does the exercises on the second page:

String Quartet

③ Look at this chart, and complete the sentences below with IS, ARE, WAS (NOT), WERE, and other words and information from the chart.

	In 1987			NOW
Jane Segall	1st violin	22	student	architect
Peter Jimson	2nd violin	22	student	engineer
Brian Cooley	viola	32	actor	TV producer
Marianne Wells	Cello	25	housewife,	music student

1 In 1987 Brian Cooley.........the viola player. He..........32 years old. He..........an actor.
2 Now he.**42**.. ....years old, and he...**15**...a TV producer.
3 In 1987 Peter Jimson..........a..........player. ....
   He.......... ....
4 Now.......... ...., and.......... ....
5 In 1987 Jane and Peter..........violin players. They...........22 years old. They..........students.
6 Now they.......... ....years........... . Jane.......... ....architect and Peter.......... ....engineer.
7 How old..........Marianne Wells in 1987?
   She.......... ....old.
8 And........... she a music student at that time?
   No, she.............. . She............ a ....

It's a Mad, Mad World: Retired Professionals!

④ Complete these "Heavenly" dialogues.

Angel	"When you were on earth, Helen, what were you?"
Helen	"I .... an architect."
Angel	"Oh, ...n't you a lawyer?"
Helen	"No, Dorothy, I .... a lawyer."
Angel	"Right. And .... you a good architect, Helen?"
Helen	"Oh yes, very, very good!"

Angel	"And what ...., Samuel?"
Samuel	"............. .... hairdresser."
Angel	"Oh, ...n't .... newsagent?"
Samuel	"No, Edward, ... a newsagent."
Angel	"Right. And .... good hairdresser, Samuel?"
Samuel	"Oh yes, very, very good!"

7

Choose the units you want to do each day.
Don't start at the beginning.

Write the exercises out in your notebook.
It is good practice for you.

Say the sentences aloud.
(You can listen to the cassette and even record your own voice.)

GOOD LUCK!

•TABLE OF CONTENTS•

Introduction						**iii**

PRESENTATION and EXERCISES

BE am is are (present tense – 1)

Look at these pictures, and study the texts.

" I am a lion tamer."

"They are lions."

"He is a clown."
Toto is a clown.

"Are you a lion tamer?"
"No, I'm not. I'm a clown."

① Now complete these sentences with AM, IS or ARE and NOT if necessary.

1   I............a writer. Fred.............a computer analyst.
2   Colin and Peter............pilots.
3   "What............you?" "I............a photographer."
4   " ....you and Sam students?" "No,............ .... We............musicians."

FORM
Affirmative
singular   *singular/plural*   *plural*
I am a secretary.   **You are** (a student, students).   **We are** Canadian.
He is a man.   **They are** French.
She is a woman.
Interrogative He→ Is he...?   **Is she** a doctor?   Where **are they**?
Negative He is→ **He is not**   **She is not** a nurse.   **They are not** here.
Contractions I am→ **I'm**   I am not→ **I'm not**
He is→ **He's**   He is not→ **He isn't**
You are→ **You're**   You are not→ **You aren't**
We say: I am cold, I am hot, I am hungry, I am thirsty, I am 25 years old. (*not:* ✗ I have cold, etc.)
We say: He is a teacher. (*not:* ✗ He is teacher.) They are students.

Good English?

② Look at the <u>underlined</u> parts of these sentences. Four of them are correct and four are wrong.
Tick (✓) the correct ones, and rewrite the wrong ones.

.... 1 <u>She not is</u> a cook.
.... 2 <u>They are</u> waiters.
.... 3 <u>Is he</u> French?
.... 4 <u>They is</u> ready

.... 5 <u>We are</u> early.
.... 6 <u>She doesn't</u> a tall girl.
.... 7 <u>You are</u> from Japan?
.... 8 <u>Is he</u> from Scotland?

My Family

③ Complete these with AM/IS/ARE and NOT; use HE/SHE/THEY if necessary.

1   I............an accountant; I............ .... a cleaner!
2   My father's first name............Dennis; ....a lawyer.
3   My mother............ ....a lawyer; ....a secondary school teacher.
4   "My grandparents............Scottish."
    " ....from Edinburgh?"
    "No,............. ....from Glasgow."
5   And my name.............Robert.

Professions

④ Complete with AM, IS or ARE and A/AN if necessary.

1   I .... doctor.
2   You .... hairdresser.
3   He .... actor.
4   She .... lawyer
5   He .... architect.
6   She .... estate agent.
7   They .... dentists.
8   You .... students.
9   I .... teacher.
10 We .... men and women.

Feelings

⑤ Write short sentences about these people.

Example:
A   *They're tired.*
B   *Are they tired?*   *Yes, they are.*

1   A ....
    B Is he thirsty?   No, he isn't. He's hungry.

2   A ....
    B .... cold?   ....

3   A ....
    B .... sad?   ....

4   A ....
    B .... hungry?   ....

5   A ....
    B .... pleased?   ....

BE am is are (present tense – 2 more practice)

Professions

① Complete these dialogues, as in the example (use A/AN if necessary).

Example:
.....*Is*..... she a nurse?
No, ...*she's*... ...*not*...; ...*she's*... .....*a*..... doctor.

1 .... he a civil engineer?
   No, ...; .... architect.
2 .... she a secretary?
   No, ...; .... systems analyst.
3 .... they company employees?
   No, ...; .... consultants.
4 .... she a housewife?
   No, ...; .... textbook writer.
5 .... they carpenters?
   No, ...; .... painters
6 .... he an office worker?
   No, ...; .... cleaner.
7 .... you a lion tamer?
   No, ...; ....

Doctors and Patients

② Complete with a form of BE, in affirmative, interrogative or negative, and a pronoun (he, you, it, etc.)
if necessary.

1 "Excuse me, ... Dr Wilson?"
   "No, ... Dr Smith. Dr Wilson .... in room 603."

2 "Excuse me, ... Dr Wilson here, please?"
   "No, ... in room 603."

3 "............. this room 603?"
   "No, ... room 604."
   "Oh, ... sorry."

4 "Excuse me, ... Dr Wilson here, please?"
   "Yes, ... over there, in the corner."

5 "Oh, good. Excuse me, ... Dr Wilson?"
   "Yes, ..."
   "Thank goodness!"

6 "And who ....?"
   "My name .... Samantha Nolan.
   ....your new assistant."

Animals, Plants and Metals

③ Complete the following sentences with words from the boxes.

| _____ is (not) | .... an animal a plant a metal |
| _____ are (not) | .... animals plants metals |

Examples:
A tiger ___is___ an animal.
Gold _is not_ a plant; it is *a mineral*.

1 Trees _____ ....
2 "_____ silver an animal?" "No, it _____; it _____ ...."
3 Dogs _____ ....
4 Flowers _____ animals; they _____ ....
5 "_____ cats ....?" "Yes, they _____."
6 Iron _____ ....
7 A horse _____ ....
8 Lead and zinc _____ ....
9 A rose _____ a metal; it _____ ....
10 "What _____ a camel?" "It _____ a plant; it _____ ...."
11 A cabbage _____ an animal; it _____ ...."
12 _____ cows plants?" "No, they _____ ; they _____ ...."
13 "_____ gold ....?" "Yes, it _____ "

Nationalities

④ Complete the following with words from the boxes.

_____ am	.............German	.............Japanese
_____ is	.............English	.............Spanish
_____ are	.............French	.............Russian

A   "Good morning. My name _____ Peter; I _____ from London. I _____ ....
Where _____ you from?"
"I _____ from Tokyo."
"Oh. _____ you ....?"
"Yes, I _____ ."

B   1   Pierre _____ ....; he _____ from Paris.
Ivan _____ French; he _____ .... He _____ from Moscow.
2   Costas _____ Greek; he _____ from Athens.
Juan _____ Greek; he _____ .... He _____ from Madrid.
3   Dieter and Hans _____ .... They _____ from Berlin.
They _____ American.
4   The two girls _____ from Liverpool. They _____ ....

C   "Hello, I _____ from Athens. I _____ .... _____ you French?
"No, we _____ from Madrid; we _____ ...."

BE was were (past tense)

Study the text, notice the date (the year 1000), and look at the picture.

At 8 am on June 1st in the year 1000....
Where was the Queen? And where were the princesses?

The Queen was in bed.   *Her daughters were in the garden.*
The King wasn't in bed.

① Now complete these with the words from the box.

was	were
wasn't	weren't

1   The King..........in the kitchen.
2   ....the boys in the garden? No, they .... .They were on the roof of the palace.
3   Where..............the Queen? She............in the kitchen; she..............in bed.
4   The girls.............in the kitchen; they............in the garden.

FORM

Affirmative

singular	*singular/plural*	*plural*
I was a baby.	**You were** (a child, children).	**We were** boys.
He was a nice boy.		**They were** girls.
She was a lovely girl.		

Interrogative

Was she a doctor?

Where **were they** yesterday?

Negative

She **was not** a nurse.

They were not here last night.

See also notes for BE in Unit 1

Good English?

② Look at the underlined parts of these sentences. Four of them are correct and four are wrong.
Tick (✔) the correct ones, and rewrite the wrong ones.

.... 1   <u>He were</u> in the garden.
.... 2   <u>Was he</u> on the roof?
.... 3   <u>We were</u> in the room.
.... 4   <u>They wasn't</u> in the kitchen.

.... 5   <u>He didn't was</u> there.
.... 6   <u>I was</u> here.
.... 7   <u>Did you were</u> at home?
.... 8   <u>She wasn't</u> in the house.

String Quartet

③ Look at this chart, and complete the sentences below with IS, ARE, WAS (NOT), WERE, and other words and information from the chart.

	In 1987			NOW
Jane Segall	1st violin	22	student	architect
Peter Jimson	2nd violin	22	student	engineer
Brian Cooley	viola	32	actor	TV producer
Marianne Wells	Cello	25	housewife	music student

1 In 1987 Brian Cooley.........the viola player. He..........32 years old. He...........an actor.
2 Now he......... ....years old, and he...........a TV producer.
3 In 1987 Peter Jimson...........a..........player. ....
    He........... ....
4 Now........... ...., and........... ....
5 In 1987 Jane and Peter.............violin players. They...........22 years old. They...........students.
6 Now they.......... ....years........... . Jane.......... ....architect and Peter.......... ....engineer.
7 How old..........Marianne Wells in 1987?
    She.......... ....old.
8 And........... she a music student at that time?
    No, she............. . She............ a ....

It's a Mad, Mad World: Retired Professionals!

④ Complete these "Heavenly" dialogues.

Angel   "When you were on earth, Helen, what were you?"
Helen   "I .... an architect."
Angel   "Oh, ...n't you a lawyer?"
Helen   "No, Dorothy, ... a lawyer."
Angel   "Right. And .... you a good architect, Helen?"
Helen   "Oh yes, very, very good!"

Angel   "And what ...., Samuel?"
Samuel   "............. .... hairdresser."
Angel   "Oh, ...n't .... newsagent?"
Samuel   "No, Edward .... newsagent."
Angel   "Right. And .... good hairdresser, Samuel?"
Samuel   "Oh yes, very, very good!"

BE and HAVE

Look at these pictures, and study the texts.

He's having a meal.
He often has a drink there.
He's having a good time.

I'M HUNGRY
I'M THIRSTY
I'M HOMELESS
I'M COLD
(AND I'M 16 YEARS OLD)

I'm hungry,
I'm thirsty,
I'm homeless,
I'm cold (and I'm 16 years old).

① Now complete these sentences with a verb from the box.

is	has	have
is having	am having	

1   It's raining, and John .... wet.
2   Sue .... a wonderful time at the disco; she .... a very good dancer.
3   Johnny .... a bath every night; he .... 4 years old.
4   I usually .... coffee in the morning, but I .... tea today.

USE

A   We use **BE** with adjectives:

She is cold.	She is strong.
He is hot.	He is nice.
She is thirsty.	She is ready.
He is hungry.	

We use **BE** for age:

He is young.   She is old.
                 She is nineteen years old.
                 She is nineteen.

B   We use **HAVE** for eating and drinking:
I have coffee in the mornings.
She doesn't have breakfast.
Let's have a drink.
Will you have tea?

We use **HAVE** for some activities:
Did you have a shower?
I am having a good time.
I had a haircut.

Good English?

② Look at the underlined parts of these sentences. Three of them are correct and three are wrong. Tick (✔) the correct ones, and rewrite the wrong ones.

.... 1   <u>We aren't</u> cold.
.... 2   <u>I have</u> hot.
.... 3   <u>She has</u> 16-years old.
.... 4   <u>They had</u> a long walk.
.... 5   <u>Did he have</u> a haircut?
.... 6   <u>He doesn't be</u> English.

③ You have to do two things: (1) complete these sentences with AM, IS, ARE, WAS, WERE, HAVE, HAS or HAD; (2) tick (✔) the sentences where you can easily use either the present tense or the past tense.

1 _____ We............. dinner at eight yesterday evening.
2 _____ She............. hungry.
3 _____ I .... 23 years old last Saturday.
4 _____ They usually .... a bath in the evening.
5 _____ We .... early for class this morning.
6 _____ We .... a good time last night.
7 _____ It .... hot today – and I .... hot!
8 _____ This child .... a temperature.
9 _____ Look at the time; they .... late again.
10 _____ I .... very tired last week.
11 _____ He .... coffee for breakfast every day.
12 _____ The weather .... very nice today.
13 _____ I .... cereal for breakfast most days.
14 _____ The twins .... six years old today.
15 _____ They .... thirsty last night.
16 _____ We .... tea with the Johnsons last weekend.
17 _____ The Johnsons usually .... lunch at home.
18 _____ I .... cold.

④ Complete these dialogues, using BE or HAVE and a word or phrase from the boxes.

> 14 years old
> cup of tea   cold

1 "............. ...."
  "Come and sit near the fire."
2 "Can .... a ....?"
  "Yes, of course; I'll give you a cup now."
3 "John ...."
  "He is tall for his age, isn't he?"

> how old/Robert
> shower   thirsty

4 "Where is Sue?"
  "............. .... in the .... "
5 "............. .... "
  "Can I get you a glass of water?"
6 "............. .... ?"
  "He's 26."

> lunch
> hungry   drink

7 "Let's .... a .... !"
  "What a good idea!"

8 "............. you ....?"
  "Yes, I'd like to eat something."
9 "Robert's not in his office."
  "It's one o'clock. He .... probably still at ...."

9

HAVE and HAVE GOT

Look at the picture, and study the texts.

She's having a meal.
She often has a drink there.
Is she having a good time? Yes!

She's got a gold watch.
Has she got a nice suit? Yes!
She hasn't got a dog.

① Now complete these sentences with a form of HAVE or HAVE GOT.

1   He .... a dog.
2   He .... a watch.
3   He .... a meal.
4   "............. he .... a drink?" "Yes."
5   "............. he .... a good time?" "No!"

USE
A   We use **HAVE** for eating, drinking and ordering food: (See Unit 4)

A   We use **HAVE** for eating, drinking and ordering food: (See Unit 4)
    He had a cup of tea.
    I'll have haddock and chips, please.

We also use **HAVE** for some activities: (See Unit 4)
    She's having a shower/bath/wash.
    He's having a shave/haircut.
    I am having a good time.

B   We use **HAVE GOT** for possession:

Affirmative	**Interrogative**	**Negative**
I have got £10.	Have you got a car?	He hasn't got time.

Good English?

② Look at the <u>underlined</u> parts of these sentences. Three of them are correct and three are wrong.
Tick (✔) the correct ones, and rewrite the wrong ones.

.............1   Carol <u>has got</u> a shower every morning.
.............2   Robert <u>has got</u> a new car.
.............3   Jimmy <u>doesn't have</u> lunch at home.
.............4   "What <u>will you have</u> for breakfast?"
.............5   "<u>I've got</u> egg and bacon, please."
.............6   "<u>I've got</u> a good time at your party."

③ Complete these sentences with a form of HAVE or HAVE GOT.
   Use HAVE GOT if possible.

   1 They .... tea in the afternoon.
   2 Fred is late this morning; he .... not .... time for breakfast.
   3 Fanny .... a car, but she .... not .... a bicycle.
   4 He always .... a bath in the evenings.
   5 Would you like to .... some orange juice first?
   6 The Johnsons .... a new dining room table.
   7 We .... lunch in a nice restaurant yesterday.
   8 The children .... an ice cream; let them finish.
   9 Look, Robert .... some new shoes.
   10 Winston .... a good time in the park last Sunday.

④ Complete these sentences using a *PRESENT* tense form of HAVE or HAVE GOT.

   1 Sue .... a wonderful time at the disco; she .... a very nice partner.
   2 John .... a walk, but he's wet because he .... not .... a raincoat.
   3 I usually .... coffee in the morning, but I .... tea today.
   4 "Are you in bed?" "Yes, I .... a rest."
   5 "Can you help me?" "Sorry, I .... not .... time."

It's a Mad, Mad World!

⑤ What's wrong with these sentences and pictures? (One is right.) Correct the sentence, or say why
   the illustration is wrong.

Oh look, John is having some tea,
and he's got some coffee.

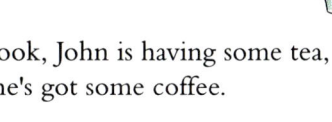

Sammy is 30 years old,
and he's got 10 years.

Jimmy has got 10 years.

6 HE WORKS   HE DOESN'T WORK (present simple - 1)

Look at the picture, and study the text.

This is Ophelia. Ophelia is a fish.
She lives in a bowl.
She doesn't eat meat; she eats fish food.
And she doesn't like Sally!

① Now complete these sentences with the verbs in the box.

eat	like
	live

This is Sally. Sally .... with a family. She .... fish food, but she .... cat food. And she .... Winston! (Winston is the dog.)

USE
We use the present simple tense when

A Something is always true:
   The earth goes round the sun.

B Something is permanent:
   Victoria lives with her husband Dennis.

FORM

Affirmative	Negative	3rd person singular
He eats She eats	He doesn't eat She doesn't eat	she eats he lives
(eat + s)	(DOESN'T + eat) (doesn't = does not)	he catches she goes

Good English?

② Look at the <u>underlined</u> parts of these sentences. Four of them are correct and four are wrong.
Tick (✔) the correct ones, and rewrite the wrong ones.

.... 1 <u>He doesn't go</u> to his office in the evening.
.... 2 <u>He go</u> to his office in the morning.
.... 3 <u>She not play</u> tennis well.
.... 4 <u>He plays</u> football on Saturdays.
.... 5 <u>She walks</u> home from work.
.... 6 <u>She doesn't walks</u> home in winter.
.... 7 <u>He don't wear</u> a suit to the office.

True or False?

③ Look at this picture of an office, then read the six sentences below the picture.

Three of these sentences are true and three are false. Mark each sentence T (true) or F (false).

		T	F
1	Susan Maintree works hard.	☐	☐
2	Mr Smithers likes Tom.	☐	☐
3	Tom Wilkes works hard.	☐	☐
4	Mr Smithers works, but not hard.	☐	☐
5	Tom Wilkes doesn't like Susan.	☐	☐
6	Susan sits at her desk all day.	☐	☐

Rewrite the false sentences, and make them true.

Affirmative

④ Complete each sentences with one of the verbs in the box, in the affirmative.

Example: **Carol eats breakfast at 7 o'clock.**

1 She .... the bus at 8.25.
2 She usually .... at 9 o'clock.
3 She .... Spanish and Italian at university.
4 In the evening she often .... television.
5 At the weekend she sometimes .... to the cinema.
6 She and Robert .... tennis together on Saturdays.

watch	play	arrive
study	go	catch

Negative

⑤ Complete each sentence with one of the verbs, in the negative.

Example: **Ophelia doesn't like cats.**

go	live	eat	speak
work	play	watch	catch

1 The baby .... to school..
2 Ophelia .... television.
3 The baby .... in a bowl.
4 Ophelia .... football.
5 Winston .... in an office.
6 The baby .... cat food.
7 Winston .... mice.
8 The baby .... Spanish.

I LIVE THEY DON'T LIVE DO YOU LIVE? (present simple – 2)

Look at the picture, and study the text. Robert is talking about his life.

Robert	*I live here with my parents.*
	Uncle Victor and Auntie Mabel don't live here.
(friend)	*Where do they live?*
Robert	*In Hampton.*
(friend)	*Does Fred live with you?*
Robert	*Yes, he does*

① Now put the verb in the correct form.

LIVE	1	.... Tom .... near the office? Yes, he does.
DRIVE / WALK	2	He .... not .... to the office; he ....
GO	3	Tom and Susan .... to the shops on Saturdays.
WORK	4	They .... not .... on Saturdays.
PLAY	5	"............ they .... tennis on Saturdays?" "Sometimes."

FORM

Affirmative	Negative	Interrogative
I You We They } **live**	I You We They } **don't live**	Do We They } **you live?**
He She It } **lives**	He She It } **doesn't live**	He Does It } **she live?**

(don't = do not)
(doesn't = does not)

Good English?

② Look at the underlined parts of these sentences. Five of them are correct and five are wrong.
Tick (✔) the correct ones, and rewrite the wrong ones.

.... 1 <u>Pete go</u> to the factory every morning.
.... 2 <u>They</u> sometimes <u>go</u> to the cinema on Fridays.
.... 3 <u>Does he play</u> squash on Wednesday nights?
.... 4 <u>Study they</u> accountancy?
.... 5 <u>They doesn't get up</u> early on Sundays.
.... 6 <u>I don't</u> often <u>visit</u> Peter and Samantha.
.... 7 <u>Samantha and Peter walk</u> to work.
.... 8 <u>Peter likes</u> Samantha? Yes, he does.
.... 9 <u>She not goes</u> to the office of Saturdays.
............10 <u>Do I look</u> well?

③ Look at the table, then complete the sentences below it.

	HOME	TRANSPORT	WORK	BEGIN WORK	FINISH WORK
Fiona	North Mimms		an office	9.30 am	5.30 pm
John	Chelsea		a school	8.30 am	3.45 pm
Tessa	Wimbledon		a factory	7 am	3 pm
Richard and Mary	Bexhill		a shop	11 am	7 pm

Example:

Fiona lives in North Mimms. Does she work in a school? No, she works in an office. She goes to work by car. She begins work at 9:30 am, but she doesn't finish at 5pm. She finishes at 5:30.

1   John .... in North Mimms; he .... in Chelsea. .... he .... in a school? Yes, and he .... to school by bus. He .... at 9.30, he .... at 8.30, and he .... at 3.45.

2   Tessa .... in Wimbledon. She .... in a factory. She .... to work by bus, she .... by train. .... she .... work at 8 am? No, she .... work at 7 am, and she .... at 3 pm.

3   Richard and Mary .... in Bexhill; they .... in a shop. .... they .... to work by car? No, they .... downstairs to the shop! They .... at 11 am and .... at 7 pm. They .... early, they .... late.

It's a Mad, Mad World!

④ Look at this picture carefully; it contains four mistakes. Complete the sentences with verbs from the box.

live	grow
have	eat

A   *The Mistakes*
Elephants .... small ears.
Lions .... bananas.
Penguins .... in Africa.
Money .... on trees.

B   *The Corrections*
Elephants .... big ears.
Lions .... meat.
Penguins .... in the Antarctic.
Money .... with interest!

HE DOES HE DOESN'T DOES HE? - (present simple – 3 more practice)

Here are two situations to practise the present simple. The first one is about Stan Wilson and Michael Hamilton. The second one is about science.

A Bus Driver and an Airline Pilot

① Read these paragraphs and complete them, using words from the box. Then complete the questions and answers following.

A Stan Wilson .... a bus for London Transport Ltd, and Michael Hamilton .... a plane for Trans European Airlines. Stan .... near the bus station, so he .... to work, but Michael .... walking, and it's a long way to the airport, so he .... the company bus.

1 a .... Stan .... a plane?
   b No, he .... a plane; he .... a bus.
2 a .... Michael .... to work?
   b No, he .... to work; he .... the company bus.

like	drive
walk	take
live	fly

B Michael and his crew .... thousands of miles every day, but Stan .... very far; he .... from Hampstead to Victoria and back. He .... about 30 times on the journey for the passengers to get on and off. Sometimes the younger passengers .... for their tickets, and that's a problem!

1 a .... Michael and his crew .... far?
   b Yes, they .... a long way.
2 a .... Stan .... far?
   b No, he .... far.

drive	travel
fly	pay
stop	

C For Stan each journey .... about an hour. They .... him a break every two hours for a few minutes. Most of the drivers .... tea in their break, but Stan .... tea. He .... coffee.

1 a How long .... each journey .... ?
   b It .... about an hour.
2 a .... the drivers .... coffee in their break?
   b No, most of them .... tea.

give	take
prefer	like
drink	

D On short flights (45 minutes to an hour), Michael .... a break; he .... in the pilot's seat all the time. The chief steward usually .... him a cup of coffee after 30 minutes' flying. On long flights he .... up every two hours. Sometimes he .... to the lavatory, and sometimes he .... to the passengers for a few minutes.

1 .... he .... up on short flights? No, he doesn't.
2 What .... the chief steward .... him? A cup of coffee.
3 Who .... Michael .... to? The passengers.

give	take
sit	talk
go	get

Science: How Much Do You Know?

② Complete these questions, using a form of DO and the verb from the answer.

1 How many times .... the earth .... every 24 hours?
   It turns once!
2 How long .... the earth .... to go round the sun?
   It takes a year.
3 How long .... bears .... in the winter?
   They sleep for about 5 months.
4 How often .... a big snake .... ?
   He eats once every two or three days.
5 How often .... cows .... ?
   They eat all the time!

③ Complete these sentences about science with the verbs given.

GO .... the sun and the moon .... the earth? The moon .... round the earth, but the sun .... round the earth.

FALL .... heavy things and light things .... at different speeds? No, they all .... at the same speed.

EAT .... a bee .... honey? No, a bee .... honey; people .... honey!

BREATHE .... whales and sharks .... air? Whales .... air, but sharks .... air.

BOIL On a mountain 2100 metres high, at what temperature .... water .... ? It .... at .... degrees Centigrade. (100? 98? 93? 85?)

④ Complete these questions and answers with suitable verbs in the present simple.

1 Where .... birds .... in the European winter? They .... south to warmer climates.
2 .... they .... across the Atlantic? Some of them .... across the Atlantic, and others .... to Africa.
3 Where .... the Inuit people .... ? They .... in Northern Canada, Alaska and Greenland.
4 What .... a squirrel .... in the autumn?   It .... nuts for the winter.

Your Life

⑤ Now write questions about yourself and your family or friends, using words and expressions from the box and words of your own.

1 Where .... you .... ? I .... in a flat/house with _____ .
2 What .... you .... ? I work/study/stay _____ .
3 What .... your brother/mother/friend etc _____ .
4 My _____ .... in/at _____ .
5 My _____ .... in/at _____ .
6 My _____ (not) .... in/at _____ .
7 My _____ (not) .... in/at _____ .

work	at home
live	in school/
study	university
do	in an office/
stay	factory

THEY ARE TALKING (present continuous)

Look at the picture, and study the texts.

Carol is washing her hands. Robert isn't washing his hands; he's combing his hair.

Carol	*Robert, what are you doing?*
Robert	*I'm combing my hair. Are you ready?*
Carol	*No, I'm washing my hands.*
Robert	*Don't be long. We must go to the theatre.*

Robert and Carol are acting in a play every night this week. Robert is playing Macbeth and Carol is playing Lady Macbeth.

① Now look at the texts again and complete these sentences using the verbs given.

1   COMB .... Robert .... his hair?   2 PLAY Robert .... Lady Macbeth;
     Yes, he is.   he .... Macbeth.

FORM		
I'm going	**He isn't going**	**Is he going?**

Spelling:

stand	standing		write –e writing		sit +t sitting
wait	waiting				swim +m swimming
look	looking				

② Now add *-ing* to these words.

sing ....   put ....   play ....   cut ....   jump ....
prepare ....   speak ....   type ....   file ....   stop ....

Good English?

③ Look at the <u>underlined</u> parts of these sentences. Five of them are correct and four are wrong. Tick (✔) the correct ones, and rewrite the wrong ones.

.... 1   <u>I am working</u> in a factory these days.
.... 2   <u>Julia is study</u> French.
.... 3   <u>Peter and John are living</u> at home.
.... 4   <u>Are Mary and Diana living</u> with you? Yes, they are.
.... 5   Where <u>Peter is working</u>? In the city.
.... 6   Where <u>are you going</u>? Home.
.... 7   <u>Peter is working</u> now? No, he isn't.
.... 8   <u>Mary and Diana are studying.</u>
.... 9   <u>You not are listening</u> to me!

At This Moment or In This Period

Study these sentences.

> *Hello, George. What are you going?*   (At this moment)
> *I am washing the car.*   (At this moment)
> *Are you still studying languages?*   (In this period)
> *Yes, I'm studying Russian.*   (In this period)

④ Now look at these sentences and say whether they are *At this moment* or *In this period*

	At this moment	In this period
1 Look at Sam; he's driving the car alone.	....	....
2 George is studying maths this year.	....	....
3 Is Sam still taking driving lessons?	....	....
4 The President is walking up the steps.	....	....

⑤ Look at this picture. What is happening?
Complete the sentences with verbs from the box.

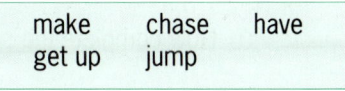

make	chase	have
get up	jump	

It is 8 o'clock in the morning. (1)Carol .... a shower and Fred .... (2)Winston
.... a lot of noise because he .... the cat around the room. (3)The two animals ....
all over the furniture.

⑥ Complete this passage with words from the box.

attack	throw	paint
do	climb	compose

Interviewer	Can you tell the television audience about your work, Julius Markham?
JM	Yes, certainly. I .... a large picture about the French Revolution. As you can see, the soldiers .... the people behind the barricades, and some young people .... the trees on the right. The man in a yellow shirt .... stones at the soldiers.
Interviewer	Yes, er, very interesting, Mr Markham. And .... you .... anything else?
JM	Yes, I .... the music for Toliatov's next film. I have many talents you see.

SHE TAKES or SHE IS TAKING (present simple or present continuous)

Look at these pictures, and study the texts.

Victoria Johnson is ironing.
Dennis Johnson is hoovering.

They both read a lot.

"What are you doing these days?"
"I'm studying European law."

They come here every day.

① Now complete the sentences with a present tense of a verb in the box.

sit	go	water	take
have	study	read	

  1 Robert ....an exciting book .
  2 Carol .... the plants every day.
  3 They .... to the theatre quite often.
  4 "And .... John still .... medicine?"
     "No, he .... a course for paramedics now."
  5 They .... one coffee and they .... there for two hours.

USE

We use the present continuous:
   A   For things happening NOW:
            You are reading this.
   B   For things happening FOR A SHORT PERIOD:
            I'm studying physics.

We use the present simple:
   C   For things which continue INDEFINITELY:
            Mr Jones works for the Inland Revenue.
   D   For things which are ETERNAL
            The earth goes round the sun.

Good English?

② Look at the <u>underlined</u> parts of these sentences. Three of them are correct and three of them are wrong.
   Tick (✔) the correct ones, and rewrite the wrong ones.

   1   Can you turn the television down? I <u>study</u>.
   2   The price of petrol <u>is going up</u> again.
   3   I <u>am never eating</u> fish; I'm allergic to it.
   4   He <u>always stays</u> at the Arosfa Hotel.
   5   I <u>paint</u> my room this weekend.
   6   The company <u>pays</u> salaries on the last Thursday of each month.

How Long?

③ Look at these statements. Are they:

A   True NOW?
B   True FOR A DEFINITE (SHORT) PERIOD (this week/month)?
C   True INDEFINITELY?
D   True "ETERNALLY"?

1   Lions don't eat grass.   _____
2   I'm working at Macdonald's for the time being.   _____
3   Look! That plane is taking off!   _____
4   Dr Smith works for the National Health Service. _____
5   Well, I'm leaving, goodbye.   _____
6   A dictionary gives you the meaning of words.   _____
(There are two A's, one B, one C and two D's.)

④ Now choose the correct alternative (a or b).

1   Dennis is winning the game   { a usually.
                                              b at the moment.

2   Robert runs two miles   { a nearly every day.
                                        b this morning.

3   Fred is helping his mother   { a every day.
                                             b today.

4   Uncle Victor drinks coffee   { a most mornings.
                                             b now.

5   Uncle Victor   a makes   } a cup of tea now.
                              b is making

6   Carol   a learns   } French these days.
                              b is learning

7   Water   a boils   } at 100° C at sea level.
                              b is boiling

The Johnsons' Activities

⑤ Complete this paragraph with the correct form of the verbs.

A   Dennis Johnson .... (live) in a flat near Paddington with his wife Victoria. She .... (work) in a travel agency in the station, and he .... (go) to an office in the City every day. He .... (sell) insurance. Today is Monday, but they are not in their offices; they .... (buy) a carpet for the living room.

B   On weekdays Fred .... (go) to school at 8.30, Robert .... (take) the train to college, and Uncle Victor .... (drive) to his office. But today is Sunday and they are all at home: Fred .... (watch) a film on the TV, Robert .... (read) a detective novel, and Uncle Victor .... (talk) to his sister on the telephone.

C   Carol .... (not, go) to school; she .... (go) to university. .... (she, like) university? Yes, she .... (enjoy) it very much. Today is Saturday, and she and her mother are shopping. Carol .... (buy) a new jacket, and her mother .... (help) her to choose. Carol .... (like) to go shopping with her mother.

MIXED EXERCISES (units 6–10)

She Usually... ....But Today... ...Because...

① Read these sentences, and complete each one (a) with an appropriate form of a verb from one of the boxes, and (b) with the right conclusion.

> go   wear   eat

1 Carol usually .... to college by bicycle,
   but today she .... by bus because.....
2 She usually .... blue jeans,
   but today she .... white shorts because .....
3 Carol usually .... supper at home,
   but today she .... supper with Simon because .....

A   it's his birthday.
B   it's raining.
C   she's going to play tennis.

> work   study
> sleep

4 Fred usually .... in his own bed,
   but this week he .... at his uncle's because .....
5 Robert usually .... in London,
   but this week he .... in Manchester because .....
6 Fred .... very hard most of the time,
   but this week he .... hard because .....

A   his company needs him there.
B   he's got examinations.
C   his room's being painted.

② Look at this picture and complete these sentences with a verb from the box in present simple or present continuous.

> eat   sit   lie
> look   sleep

1 The cat .... at Ophelia.
2 Winston .... about kilo of meat
   every day.
3 The cat .... about 14 hours a day.
4 Dennis .... in an armchair.
5 Winston .... on the floor.

> eat   stand   go
> live   give

6 Fred .... to school every day.
7 Ophelia .... her supper.
8 Fred usually .... Ophelia her supper.
9 Fred .... near the table.
10 Ophelia .... in a fishbowl.

Questionnaire

③ Complete these questions, and answer them. Some of them are present simple, and some are present continuous.

What's your name? ....

1	LIVE	Where .... you .... ?	....
2	WORK	Where .... you .... ?	....
3	STUDY	.... you .... ?	....
4	DO	What .... you .... at present?	....
5	SIT	Where .... you .... ?	....
6	WRITE	.... you .... this exercise with a pen or a pencil?	....
7	STUDY	.... you .... English every day?	....

Look out of the window.

8	RAIN	.... it .... ?	....
9	SHINE	.... the sun .... ?	....
10	RAIN	.... it .... usually this month?	....

Normal or Strange?

④ Do you think these sentences are "NORMAL" or "STRANGE"? Tick (✔) the normal ones (3), and rewrite the strange ones (3).

.... 1 Mum, the water is boiling!

.... 2 Water is normally boiling at 100ºC.

.... 3 "Hello, Fred, what do you do?"
"My homework."

.... 4 Peter and John travel a lot; they are salesmen.

.... 5 Cows are not eating meat this year.

.... 6 They are playing football this afternoon.

It's a Mad, Mad World!

⑤ Look at these pictures, and complete the sentences appropriately.

1 BARK
Listen to that cat! It .... !
Don't be silly; cats .... ; dogs ....

2 FLY
Look at that elephant! It .... !
Don't be silly; elephants .... ; birds .... !

3 WEAR
Look at Fred! He .... a business suit!
Don't be silly; that's not Fred. Fred ....
a school uniform.

23

HE WORKED DID HE WORK? HE DID NOT WORK
(past simple – 1)

Look at the picture, and study the texts.

From 1986 to 1988, Dennis worked in Liverpool and lived in Chester.

He did not live in London.

"Did he work in London?"
"No."

① Complete these sentences with the verbs in the boxes.

1 .... Dennis .... his father yesterday?
2 No, he .... his father.
3 He .... his mother.

VISIT	visited

4 .... Carol .... you last night?
5 No, she .... me.
6 She .... her brother Robert.

PHONE	phoned

FORM

Past tense (regular verbs):   walk   **+ ed**   walk**ed**
move   **+ d**   mov**ed**
carry -y   **+ied**   carr**ied**

Affirmative   He walk**ed** to the office yesterday.
Negative   She **did not** walk to the office yesterday.
Affirmative   He walk**ed** to the office yesterday.
Interrogative   **Did** she walk to the office yesterday **?**

For irregular verbs, see Units 13 - 14; for contractions, see Unit 14

Good English?

② Look at the underlined parts of these sentences. Three of them are correct and three are wrong. Tick (✔) the correct ones, and rewrite the wrong ones.

.... 1 <u>Did</u> you <u>wanted</u> something?
.... 2 They <u>entered</u> the house quietly
.... 3 He liked the food, but he <u>not liked</u> the wine.
.... 4 <u>Did</u> you <u>remember</u> to buy the milk?
.... 5 She <u>visit</u> me last night.
.... 6 <u>Did</u> you <u>talk</u> to your mother on the phone?

Yesterday ...

③ Complete each sentence with the past tense (affirmative) of the verb in brackets.

Example: Yesterday morning Robert ...*washed* (wash) his face.

1   He .... (dress) carefully.
2   He .... (walk) to the corner.
3   At the corner, he .... (wait) for his friend Michael.
4   His friend .... (arrive) at 8.15 am.
5   They .... (work) together from 9 to 12.

Every Day and Yesterday

④ Write the second sentence in the past tense (negative), as in the example.

Example: He usually plays chess, but yesterday ...*he didn't play chess.* ....

1   He usually likes his food, but yesterday ....
2   He usually helps his wife, but yesterday ....
3   He usually washes up after supper, but yesterday ....
4   He usually studies in the evening, but yesterday ....
5   He usually works from 9 to 5, but yesterday ....

⑤ Write a question for each answer, using the same verb as that in the answer.

Example: Where ...*did you park the car?*
                 I parked the car in the street.

1   When .... ?
    She typed the letters this morning.
2   Why .... ?
    I changed my shirt because it was dirty.
3   How much .... ?
    I saved five pounds.

4   What time .... ?
    I asked her to come at 6.30.
5   How .... ?
    I entered the house through the window.
6   When .... ?
    She arrived at 7.15.

Conversation About Cooking

⑥ Complete each sentence with the past tense of the verb in brackets.

1   What .... (you, cook) for supper last night?
2   I .... (cook) a big meal.
3   I .... (fry) the steaks in the frying pan.
4   .... (you, boil) any vegetables?
5   Yes, I .... (boil) some potatoes, but I .... (not, cook) any cabbage, because Carol doesn't like cabbage.
6   .... (prepare) a dessert?
7   Yes, but I .... (not, bake) an apple pie; I .... (serve) strawberries and cream.
8   .... (they, enjoy) the meal?
9   Well, they both said they .... (like) it a lot!

HE WOKE UP HE DIDN'T WAKE UP (past simple – 2)

Look at the picture, and study the texts.

Lesley usually wakes up early.
But this morning she did not wake up early;
she woke up late.

She did not hear her alarm clock.
She heard the postman at 8 am.

① Now complete these sentences with the verbs in the boxes.

1 a She usually drinks tea in the morning.
   b But yesterday she .... (not) tea.
   c She .... water instead.

DRINK drank

2 a She usually goes to work by bus.
   b But yesterday she .... (not) by bus
   c She .... by taxi.

GO went

FORM

Past tense *(irregular verbs, affirmative and negative)*
We form the past tense in two ways, REGULAR (see Unit 12) and IRREGULAR.
Most common verbs have irregular past tenses in English
Affirmative

Present tense
He usually **drinks** water.
I **go** to the office every day.

Past tense
On Friday he **drank** coke.
Yesterday I **went** to the office in the evening.

Negative

On Friday he drank coke.
On Thursday he didn't drink coke.

He bought a pen.
He didn't buy a pencil.

---

② Here is the first list of irregular verbs (other list on second page of Unit 14). All the past tenses are in the box. Complete the list.

begin	give	make	see	take ....
buy	go	put	sit	tell.............
come	hear	read	speak	wake.............
drink	leave	say	stand	write ....

made	sat	wrote	stood	read	gave	began	left	told	went
spoke	bought	drank	woke	took	said	saw	put	heard	came

Good English?

③ Read these sentences; they are all in the past tense. Four of the <u>underlined</u> parts are correct and four are wrong. Tick (✔) the correct ones, and rewrite the wrong ones.

.... 1 <u>Carol spoke</u> to Robert.
.... 2 <u>She not went</u> to his room.
.... 3 <u>She putted</u> a tape on her cassette recorder.
.... 4 <u>Carol wrote</u> some letters.
.... 5 <u>Robert didn't wrote</u> any letters.
.... 6 <u>Robert didn't see</u> Carol.
.... 7 <u>He heard</u> her voice.
.... 8 <u>She not made coffee; she made</u> tea.

④ Complete these sentences with the past tense of the verb (some are negative).

1	PUT/SIT	She .... the bottle on the table and .... down.
2	WAKE/GIVE	They .... the baby up and .... her the bottle.
3	STAND/LEAVE	He .... up and .... the room.
4	COME/BEGIN	Uncle Victor .... into the room and .... to dance.
5	BUY/DRINK	He .... a coke, but it was warm and he .... (not) .... it.
6	SEE/SPEAK	He .... Susan but he .... (not) .... to her.
7	MAKE/TELL	Carol .... some scrambled eggs, and .... Jimmy to eat them.
8	SAY/GO	He .... "goodbye" and .... home.
9	TAKE/READ	Tom .... a book with him, but he .... (not) .... it.
10	WRITE/POST	He .... a letter to Carol, but he .... (not) .... it.

⑤ Choose the right verb in the box, and complete the sentences with the past tense (some are negative).

begin	take	come
make	sit	say

1   Yesterday morning Helen Grey .... (not) .... into her office at 9.00; she was late.
She arrived at 9.20. She .... (not) .... hello to Patty, who is her secretary.
She .... off her coat and .... down. Then she ....to work.
First, she .... a plan for the day.

give	read	write
speak	tell	

2   Then she .... a letter to her boss. She .... him she was not pleased with the new
office hours. She .... (not) .... letter to Patty, but she typed it herself. ·Then she
.... a report from the sales department, and .... to three people on the telephone.

see	leave
stand	buy

3   At eleven o'clock she .... up and .... the room. In the cafeteria she .... a cup
of coffee; then she .... an old friend who was sitting at a table.

DID SHE WAKE UP? (past simple – 3)

Look at these pictures, and study the texts.

"*Did Lesley wake up early yesterday?*"
"*No, she didn't.*"

"*Did she hear her alarm clock?*"
"*No, she didn't.*"
"*Did she hear the postman?*"
"*Yes, she did.*"

① Now complete these sentences with appropriate forms of the two verbs.

1   "............. she .... tea yesterday?"
     No, she didn't. She .... water."

DRINK drank

2   "............. she .... to the office by bus?"
     No, she didn't . She .... by taxi."

GO   went

3   "............. she .... to the office early?"
     No, she didn't. She .... there late."

GET   got

4   "............. she .... her boss a lie?"
     "No, she didn't. She .... him the truth."

TELL told

FORM

Past tense (irregular/irregular + interrogative)

Affirmative	*Interrogative*
He drank water on Monday.	**Did he drink** coke on Tuesday?
It rained yesterday.	**Did it rain** last night?

Past tense (summary)

	Affirmative	*Negative*	*Interrogative*
Irregular verbs	She left.	She did not leave.	Did she leave?
Regular verbs	She walked.	She did not walk.	Did she walk?

Writing (usually): did not
Speaking (usually): didn't

② Here is list number two of irregular verbs (the other list is on the first page of Unit 13). Complete it from the box.

slept	drove	ran	got	spent (on)	ate	paid (for)	knew	did	meant
learnt	taught	had	wore	understood	cost	thought	sold	met	

cost .... have .... pay .... teach ....

do .... know .... run .... think ....

drive .... learn .... sell .... understand ....

eat .... mean .... sleep .... get ....

meet .... spend .... wear ....

③ Complete these sentences with appropriate forms of the verbs used.

1 Did Jimmy run in the first race?
No, he .... in the first race; he .... in the second race.

2 .... Carol .... the answer to the first question?
No, she didn't know the answer to the first one, but she .... the answer to the second one.

3 .... Robert .... a bicycle for his birthday?
No, he .... a bicycle; he got a motorcycle.

4 Did the cinema cost much?
No, the cinema .... much, but the supper .... a lot!

④ You have to write questions. The important part of each answer is in **bold.**

1 .... ?
Yes, Robert went to his office yesterday.

2 .... ?
Carol got up **at seven o'clock** this morning.

3 .... ?
No, Uncle Victor didn't buy a new car.

4 .... ?
Yes, Sally wanted to eat Ophelia.

5 .... ?
Yes, Carol spent all her money.

It's a Mad, Mad World!

⑤ Read the first four sentences. Are they true? Correct them. (Be careful; one is correct!) Then complete the last four sentences and answer them.

1 Columbus went to America in 1642.
2 The Second World War started in 1933.
3 Roman soldiers wore short skirts.
4 Shakespeare knew Beethoven.

5 Before Columbus, ... people .... (think) the world was flat?........................
6 .... Plato ....(speak) English?..
7 .... Cleopatra .... (drive) a car?..
8 .... Attila the Hun .... (visit) England? ....

Multilevel Eng. Gr. programme.

HE DID HE DIDN'T DID HE? (past simple – 4 more practice)

① In each item, the same verb is used three times. We have used it once; you have to use it twice.
(The first one has been done for you.)

1   *Did* .... you ....*drink*...... all the milk?
     No, I *didn't drink* all the milk; I drank about half of it.
2   .... Carol .... on Tuesday?
     No, she .... on Tuesday; she came on Wednesday.
3   .... they .... to the cinema on Saturday evening?
     No, they .... on Saturday evening; they went on Saturday afternoon.
4   .... the show .... at 7.30?
     No, it .... at 7.30; it was late. It began at 7.50.

② Complete these sentences with affirmative, negative or interrogative forms of the verbs given.

1   HAVE   In the morning Carol .... £10, but she .... £10 in the evening!
              How much .... she............. ? 30p
2   PAY   How much .... she .... for her Travel Card?
              She .... £2.80.
3   SPEND   How much .... she .... in the clothing store?
              She .... £7.50.
4   LEARN   What .... she .... that day?
              She .... to be careful with money!
5   MAKE   In the evening at home, she .... a cup of tea for Robert.
              But she .... not .... any for herself.

③ Read these questions. First match the answers to the questions. Then complete the answers with the same verb used in the question.

1   How much did the furniture cost? ....
2   Did Jimmy run home after school? ....
3   What did Carol wear to the office? ....
4   Didn't you understand the question? ....

     A   Yes, he .... to a friend's house.
     B   Well, the chairs .... £20 each, and the table .... £50.
     C   No, I .... not .... it, because the items were too difficult!
     D   She .... a dark suit.

5   Did Robert drive to the office? ....
6   Where did you get that hat? ....
7   When did Uncle Victor sell his old car? ....
8   Did you meet George Brown at the station? ....

     E   I .... it in a second-hand shop.
     F   He .... it last week.
     G   No, I .... n't .... George Brown; I .... George Perkins.
     H   No, he .... to the station, parked his car and took the train.

④ Complete each sentence with the correct form of the right verb from the box. Most of the verbs are regular, but some are irregular (-ed).

leave	wait	go
sleep	hear	walk

1 Fred .... to bed early, and .... for 8 hours.
   He .... the alarm clock at 6.30 am. He got up, and .... the house at 8 o'clock.
   He .... to the bus stop, and he .... for the bus.

sell	tell	cost
buy	pay	phone

2 "Robert .... his old car and .... a new one!"
   "How exciting. How do you know?"
   "He .... me yesterday and .... me."
   "How much .... the new car .... ?"
   "He .... £7000 for it."

think	mean	understand
say	teach	study

3 Carol............. in France for two months last summer. One day her French
   teacher .... the difference between *femme* and *faim*, but Carol .... not
   .... She .... the two words were the same. So before lunch she .... :
   "I have a wife!" But of course she .... to say: "I am hungry!"

jump	go	land
take	drive	

4 Dennis and Victoria .... to Greece for a week. They left home on 4th June, and at
   11 am the plane .... in Corfu. They .... to the hotel, and Dennis .... off his
   clothes and .... into the swimmimng pool!

Do/Did

Is it a main verb? Is it an auxiliary verb? Is it an infinitive?

⑤ Fill in all the blanks with DO or DID.

   "(1)............. you (2)............. all the work I asked you to (3)............. ?"
   "Well, I (4)............. some of it, but I (5)............. n't (6)............. all of it."
   "Why (7)............. n't you (8)............. the rest of it?"
   "Because I (9)............. n't have time! What (10)............. you want me to (11)............. , work
   myself to death?"

⑥ Say what each of the verbs are (the first three have been done for you.)

   a   Main verbs: 2 ....
   b   Auxiliary verbs: 1 ....
   c   Infinitives: 3 ....

HE WAS STANDING (past continuous)

Look at these pictures, and study the texts.

Victoria *What were you doing when the window broke?*
Carol   *I was playing the piano.*
Fred   *I was using my computer.*

Victoria *And what were Dennis and*
          Robert doing?
Carol   *They were playing football.*

① Now complete each sentence with a verb from the box.

have	swim
watch	do

At nine o'clock,
1   Ophelia .... round and round in her bowl.
2   Sally the cat .... her.
3   Robert .... his supper.
4   Carol and Fred .... their homework.

USE

An action in the past which was not finished:
    I was eating a banana.   (I didn't finish it.)
    (Compare: I ate a banana. (I finished it.)

FORM

Affirmative	Negative	Interrogative
I was coming.	He wasn't coming.	Were they coming?

Good English?

② Look at the underlined parts of these sentences. Three of them are correct and four of them are wrong.
Tick (✔) the correct ones, and rewrite the wrong ones.

.... 1   They was going home.
.... 2   He was not playing the violin.
.... 3   "I was wait for you."
.... 4   Were they working in the bank?
.... 5   Jim and Robert were going to the post office.
.... 6   He not was coming with us.
.... 7   He was listening to the radio?

An Explosion!

Half an hour ago, at 11.32 am, a bomb exploded in the National Bank in William Street. A police Inspector is asking questions.

③ Look at the picture, choose a character (numbers 1 to 4), and write out complete answers to the questions. (The phrases in the box below should help you.)

Where were you when the bomb exploded, sir/madam?
1 I..
And what were you doing?
    I...
2 I...........................
    and I...................
3 I...................
    and I......................
4 *He*...................
    and he......................

sitting at the computer	standing at the counter
standing near the door	sitting at my desk
answering the telephone	cashing a cheque
just coming in	putting in data

Two Suspicious Characters

④ Complete this dialogue with the past continuous of the verbs.

"Hello, is that the Wilton police station?"
"Yes, madam, can I help you?"
"Yes, I want to report a suspicious character."
"Where is he, madam?"
"I don't know where he is now, but last night he .... (stand) outside my house."
"Oh yes, madam? And what .... (he, do)?"
"He .... (talk) to another man who .... (sit) in a car. They .... (look) at the bank across the street."
"I see, madam. Can you describe them?"
"Well, the man who .... (stand) on the pavement .... (wear) a long overcoat and a black hat. The man in the car .... (not, wear) a coat, but he .... (wear) dark glasses. Why .... (he, do) that? The sun .... (not, shine); it was eleven o'clock at night! That's suspicious, isn't it? I'm sure these men were criminals!"

I WAS GOING and I WENT (past simple and past continuous)

Look at the picture, and all the things that happened.

What were you doing when the earthquake happened?

What did you do when the fire started?

① Complete the two sets of sentences with the correct tense of the verb given.

8 am …
1   When the earthquake happened, Carol (comb hair) ....
2   When the earthquake happened, Robert (have shower).............................
3   When the earthquake happened, Victoria (have breakfast)..........................
4   When the earthquake happened, Uncle Victor (make a cup of tea) ....
5   When the earthquake happened, Ophelia (swim)....................................
6   When the earthquake happened, Fred and Winston (sleep) ....

7 pm …
1   When the fire started, Carol (shout for help) ....
2   When the fire started, Robert (get hose out).....................................
3   When the fire started, Victoria (call fire brigade)................................
4   When the fire started, Uncle Victor (not notice anything)..............................
5   When the fire started, Ophelia (nothing)..
6   When the fire started, Fred and Winston (run out) ....

② Complete these sentences with the correct tense of the verbs given, past simple or past continuous.

1   Victoria called Jimmy, but he .... (watch) the television and he .... (not, hear) her.
2   When Victoria .... (come) in, Uncle Victor .... (sit) in front of the fire.
3   "I .... (buy) a new handbag this afternoon."
    "Really? How much .... (it, cost)?"
4   Uncle Victor .... (drive) home when he .... (see) an old friend of his.
5   Robert .... (wake) up at seven o'clock, and .... (put) on his clothes.
6   Jimmy .... (eat) an ice cream when Robert came up and .... (speak) to him.
7   They .... (go) to the cafe and .... (meet) Alphonse; he .... (read) the
    newspaper and .... (drink) a lemonade.

③ Choose the best (or most probable) of the two alternatives in the following sentences.

1   Carol knocked on the door, and Robert { was opening / opened } it.

2   The sun { was shining, / shone, } so we sat in the garden.

3   While Jimmy was doing the test he { was making / made } four mistakes.

4   We saw some boys in the park. They { were playing / played } football.

5   When I went into the house a dog { was biting / bit } me.

6   When we went out it { was raining. / rained. }

7   Carol waited for an hour; he { was arriving / arrived } at 8 pm.

8   Dennis phoned the house and Victoria { answered / was answering } it.

9   Fred { was watching / watched } a TV programme when Carol got home.

10 I { was reading / read } this book last night, but I didn't finish it.

④ Choose the right verb from the boxes and the right tense for each of these sentences.

sell	say
pay	understand

1   The man .... he .... not .... Russian.
2   I .... £500 for my car 10 years ago, and last week I .... it for the same amount!

leave	think
stand	begin

3   Robert .... in the street when he .... he saw Jimmy sitting in a taxi!
4   At six o'clock I .... just .... the office when it .... to rain.

take	teach	learn
wear	write	

5   Carol .... a letter in the park when a man .... her handbag.
6   Carol had a new teacher yesterday. He .... a pair of blue jeans with holes in them, but he .... a lot! She .... more that day than in the last six months.

give	spend
know	mean

7   He asked her a question, but she .... not .... what he ....
8   He wasn't very careful with his money; he .... half of it, and .... the other half to the poor.

MIXED EXERCISES (units 12 – 17)

① Complete these paragraphs with the right form of a verb from the box.

1
eat	read	get up
leave	have	

2
start	leave	
see	put	go

1 Robert .... the house at 7.45 am. At that time, Carol .... a shower, Dennis .... his breakfast in the kitchen with Victoria, who .... her newspaper. Jimmy .... just ....

2 When Robert .... the house, he .... that it .... just .... to rain, so he .... back to the house and .... on his raincoat.

② Using the same or other verbs, make questions to fit these answers.

1 .... Robert .... ?
   At 7.45 am.

2 Where .... Dennis .... ?
   In the kitchen.

3 What did Robert see when he .... the house?
   He saw it was raining.

4 What .... Robert .... then?
   He went back to get his raincoat.

③ Complete this paragraph with the right form of a verb from the box.

buy	have	stand
come	take	go

Robert .... to the underground station. He had a weekly ticket, so he .... (not) .... a ticket. He .... on the platform for five minutes, but the train .... (not) .... , so he walked to another platform and .... a different train.

④ Make questions to fit these answers.

1 .... Robert .... ?
   Because he had a weekly ticket.

2 How long .... on the platform?
   For five minutes.

⑤ Complete these paragraphs with the right form of a verb from the box.

1
say	sit	
put	come	

2
get on	pay
leave	

1 He .... on the train reading his newspaper, when an inspector .... into the carriage, and .... : "Tickets, please." Robert .... his hand in his raincoat pocket, but he could not find his ticket!

2 "I'm sorry," said Robert, "I think I .... my weekly ticket at home."
   "Where .... you .... ?" asked the inspector.
   "At Baker Street."
   "That's sixty pence."
   And Robert .... for another ticket!

⑥ Complete these paragraphs with the right form of a verb from the box.

hear	wake	sleep
say	tell	eat

A On Thursday morning Jimmy .... until 8 o'clock. Then his mother .... him up, and .... him to get dressed quickly. He .... his breakfast when he .... the announcer on the radio. The announcer .... : "There is a security alert at The Hampton secondary school; all children should stay at home this morning."

drink	have	give
go	meet	spend
walk	know	

B So Jimmy .... (not) ....to school. His mother .... him 25 pence and he .... to the shop to buy a coke when he .... his friend Sam. They .... (not) .... what to do. Sam .... (not) .... any money, so Jimmy .... the 25 pence on one coke and they .... it together.

go	drive	know
begin	stop	like

C Carol .... home in her father's car when it .... to rain. She .... (not) .... driving in the rain, but she .... (not) .... , because she .... her father wanted the car at 6 o'clock. He and Victoria .... to the cinema together at 6 o'clock.

want	speak	get
stop	say	

D But the rain .... worse, and Carol .... the car near a public telephone. She .... to her father, and .... she .... (not) .... to drive because she was nervous.

drive	watch	want
wait	rain	

E Her father said they .... a film on television, and they .... (not) .... to go to the cinema, because it .... So Carol .... in the car for 10 minutes, and then she .... home.

run	walk	remember	buy
write	have	sell	cost

F Auntie Mabel and Uncle Victor .... their big house last month, and .... a small flat. The new flat .... £40,000. UncleVictor .... a cheque for £40,000 with the money from the big house. Yesterday afternoon they .... to the new flat when Uncle Victor .... he .... (not) .... the keys. So Fred, who was with them, ... back to get the keys.

understand	stood (2)
think	teach

G One day, the maths teacher .... at the front of the class. He .... algebra. Fred .... (not) .... algebra, but he .... he did , so he .... up and answered the question. They all laughed!

37

I HAVE FINISHED (present perfect)

Look at these pictures, and study the texts.

This is Rosette.

She lived in Moscow until 1984.   *Now she lives in Miami.*

1984...NOW.....................................
She has lived in Miami since 1984.

① Now complete these sentences.

   1   I............. in Mexico until 1988.   2   Now I .... in England.
   3   I .... in London .... 1988.

USE	FORM
	We form the present perfect with HAVE + PAST PARTICIPLE. I (you, etc.) **have worked** He (she, etc.) **has done** it **Some irregular verbs**
A The present perfect JOINS the past and the present: Past tense <··············> Present tense PRESENT PERFECT	

USE

A   The present perfect JOINS the past and the present:
   Past tense <··············> Present tense
     PRESENT PERFECT

B   It joins the past and the present in two ways:
   1 The action continues from the past to the present
   I lived here. <··············> I'm living here.
      I HAVE LIVED HERE

   2 The action is past, but has an effect on the
     present:

   | SHE HAS DONE IT. | and here it is

FORM

We form the present perfect with HAVE + PAST PARTICIPLE.
I (you, etc.) **have worked**
He (she, etc.) **has done** it
Some irregular verbs

Present	Past	Past Participle
be	was/were	been
break	broke	broken
come	came	come
do	did	done
give	gave	given
go	went	gone
make	made	made
meet	met	met
see	saw	seen
sing	sang	sung
speak	spoke	spoken
take	took	taken
write	wrote	written

Good English?

② Look at the <u>underlined</u> parts of these sentences. Four of them are correct and four are wrong.
Tick (✔) the correct ones, and rewrite the wrong ones.

.... 1 <u>Peter have finished</u> supper.   .... 5 <u>He hasn't went</u> home.
.... 2 <u>They have gone</u> to the cinema, I think. .... 6 <u>Has he broken</u> his arm?
.... 3 <u>Did you have phoned</u> your sister?   .... 7 <u>John hasn't taken</u> a day off this year.
.... 4 What <u>have you done</u> to your tie?   .... 8 <u>He not has come</u> back yet.

Present Perfect

③ Complete each sentence with the correct form of the present perfect.

1 "............ (you, speak) to Mike today?"
   "No, I .... (not, see) him. I think he .... (go) to Manchester for the day."
2 "............ (Helen, type) those letters yet?"
   "She .... (do) some of them, but she .... (not, finish) them yet."
3 "............ (you, see) 'Deadly Mission'?"
   "No. I .... (see) two other films this week, but I .... (not, see) that one."
4 "............ (you, read) 'Oliver Twist'?"
   "No. I .... (read) four of Dickens' novels, but I .... (not, read) 'Oliver Twist' yet."
5 " .... (you, finish) your thesis yet?"
   "No. I .... (make) a lot of notes, but I .... (not, write) it yet."

Present or Present Perfect

④ Use each verb twice, once in the present and once in the present perfect.

LIVE   1   a) 1 .... in 160 Bedford Street.
            b) I .... here since 1963.
WORK   2   a) John Smith .... for that company since 1990.
            b) He .... in the personnel department.
GO   3   a) Same and Jane .... to the cinema on Saturday.
            b) They .... on the same day since they were children.
SEE   4   a) "............ you .... Susan this week?"
            b) "Yes, I .... her every day of my life."
BREAK   5   a) "Look, he .... another glass."
            b) "Yes, he .... one nearly every day."
COME   6   a) " .... you .... here often?"
            b) "I .... every week for the last two years."

It's a Mad, Mad World!

⑤ Use the correct form of a verb in the box to fill in the blanks.

break	give
take	kill

Mrs Mannering asked the terrible twins (Tim and Tom) to do some work for her this morning.
She came back at lunch time, and ...

"Oh my God! They .... all the furniture out of the house!
They .... the Chinese vase!
Tim .... the goldfish!
And Tom .... the whisky to the dog!"

PRESENT PERFECT/PAST + FOR...   PAST + ... AGO
(present perfect or past)

Look at this time line and read the texts.

	PAST		NOW
1970		1990	

Jack drove that old car for many years.   *He sold it
a few years ago.*

① Now complete these sentences with AGO or FOR and the phrase in brackets.

1   After a long day, I slept deeply .... (8 hours)
2   Mrs Smith arrived .... ; she likes the hotel. (2 days)
3   He sat in the chair and didn't move .... (an hour)
4   "Is it too late for the 8.45 train?"
    "Oh yes, it's 8.50 now, that train left .... (5 minutes)

Now look at this time line and study the texts.

	PAST		NOW
1970		1990	

Jack drove that old car for many years.   *He has driven his new car for a
few years (and he likes it).*

② Now complete these sentences with the past tense or the present perfect of a verb from the box.

| be   work |

1   Mrs Parker .... in a bank for five years, from 1980 to 1985.
2   He .... for an engineering firm for two years, and he's still there.
3   Her son .... at medical school for two years; he's got three more years to do.
4   He .... at secondary school for seven years before he went to university.

USE

A We use **FOR** with a PERIOD OF TIME
   a   In the past:
          I **studied** at Oxford **for three years**. (1985 - 1988)
   b   From past to present:
          I **have studied** at Oxford **for a few years**. (1991 - NOW)
          1991 <·················> NOW

B We use **AGO** with a POINT IN TIME
   In the past:
   I began to study in Oxford **a few years ago**.
   1991 <·················> NOW

Past or Present Perfect

③ Complete this dialogue with the past or the present perfect of two verbs, SEE and BE.

"Hullo, Peter! I .... not .... you for a long time!"
"Hullo, John! I .... you last six months ago, at school."
"That's right! Where .... you .... all this time?"
"I .... in London."
"Really! .... you .... Sam and Jane recently?"
"I .... not .... Sam for a year, but I .... Jane a week ago."
"Oh, did you? How is she?"
"Fine".
"Good. And .... you .... Brian?"
"No. He .... in Scotland last month. He .... there three times this year."

Today is December 31st: Reviewing the Year

④ Look at the calendar, and then complete the sentences below.

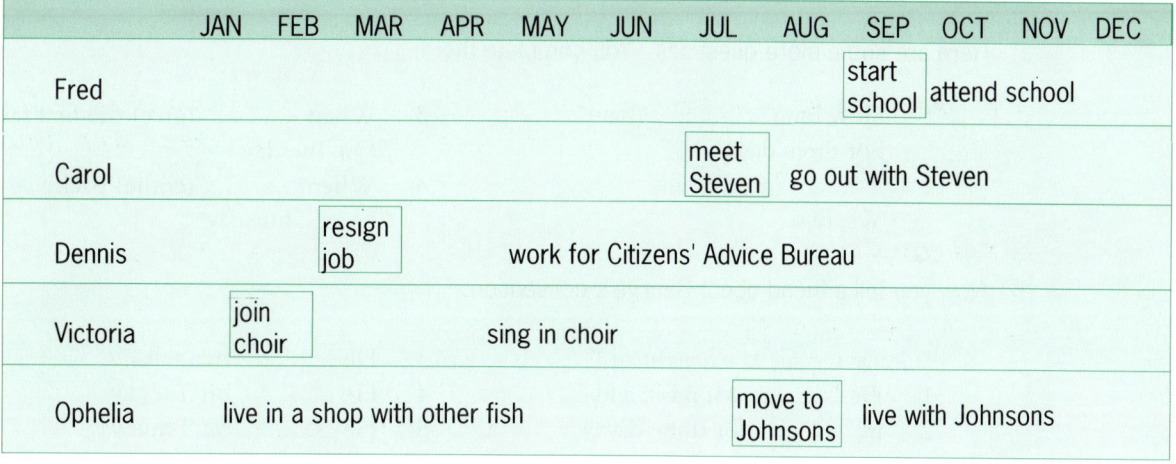

	JAN	FEB	MAR	APR	MAY	JUN	JUL	AUG	SEP	OCT	NOV	DEC
Fred									start school	attend school		
Carol							meet Steven	go out with Steven				
Dennis		resign job		work for Citizens' Advice Bureau								
Victoria	join choir				sing in choir							
Ophelia	live in a shop with other fish						move to Johnsons	live with Johnsons				

Who?

1 He _____ school for four months ....   _____
   He _____ in school .... four months.

2 She _____ a choir for eleven months.   _____
   She _____ the choir .... eleven months.

3 He _____ from his job ten months ....   _____
   He _____ for the Citizens' Advice Bureau .... ten months.

4 She _____ in a shop .... eight months.
   She _____ to the Johnsons four months ....   _____
   She _____ with the Johnsons .... four months.

5 She _____ Steven six months ....   _____
   She _____ out with Steven .... six months.

I'M LEAVING TOMORROW   (future – 1)

Look at the picture, and study the texts.

George is attending a convention next week; his friend Peter wants to know all about it.

"When are you leaving?"
"On Monday."

"Where are you staying?"
"At the Grand Hotel."

① Here are some more questions. You complete them.

1   How long .... ? (stay)
    For three days.

2   .... (give) a talk?
    Yes, two.

3   When .... (give) the first talk?
    On Tuesday.

4   When .... (come) back?
    Next Thursday.

② Now you tell a friend about George's convention.

"George is going to a convention."

1   He .... Monday, and

2   he .... for three days.

3   He .... two talks.

4   He .... on Tuesday.

5   He .... on Thursday.

USE

Present Progressive (Future)
We often use this tense to join the PRESENT and the FUTURE:

   I am flying to Tokyo on Sunday.
   John is driving to Brighton on Saturday.
   I am starting my new job next week.
   Hello, Peter, are we playing squash tonight?

All these sentences are about the plans and arrangements people make. These are all things they want to do, or perhaps have to do; the important thing is that the arrangements have now been made.
In the last example, somebody wants to confirm the arrangements.

For present continuous, see also Unit 9

FORM

(See Unit 9)

Busy Julia

③ Fran is asking Julia about her plans for the week; Julia is always busy!
Fill in what Julia says about her week.

What are your plans for the week?

1 Well, on Monday I .... (meet)
   .... at ....

2 And on Tuesday Jim and I ....
   to the cinema together.

3 Then on Wednesday I ....
   .... with my ....

4 On Thursday I ....
   at the .... , and

5 On Friday, I - Oh!

What's the matter, dear?

No, nothing. On Friday, you and I
...............................together to see ....

Yes, dear.

MONDAY	6·30 JOHN
TUESDAY	8·00 CINEMA JIM
WEDNESDAY	Supper GRANDMA
THURSDAY	See Susan CAFE
FRIDAY	"CATS"

It's a Mad, Mad World: The Frantic Executive's Day!

④ Fill in the blanks with information from the diary.

Are you busy tomorrow, Hank?

No, just normal.
   I .... at six o'clock,
   then I ....,
   then I ....,
   and at 7.25 I ....,
   then I ....
   and at 11.15 I ....
   I .... at 12.30 with ....
   and in the afternoon I ....
   to the staff at the branch office.
   Then at 4.45 I ....
   to the airport, and I ....
   I .... with my wife, and then we
   .... at my son's school.
   It's a quiet day.

You call that a quiet day?!?

FRIDAY 13th FEBRUARY

6. Breakfast

6·25. Phone Singapore

6·45. See appointments
      Secretary.

7·25. Drive to office
      meet area managers

11·15 have coffee with
      the Hong Kong rep.

12·30 Lunch with ass.
      talk to staff

4·45 Drive to airport

5·30 Meeting with
      European manager

Supper. Susan

8·30 Meeting at
     Robin's School.

I'M GOING TO DO IT (future – 2)

Look at these pictures, and study the texts.

"I'm going to have a bath."   *"What are you going to buy for dinner?"*

① Now complete these with appropriate forms of GOING TO.

1   "Have you written to your aunt?"   2   "............. (you) fly to France?"
      "No, I .... write now."   "I .... (not) fly. I .... use the new tunnel!"

USE

The "going to" future

A   We use **GOING TO** when we talk about the things we want to do or intend to do:

What are you going to do this weekend?
    I'm going to stay at a hotel in Dorset.   I'm not going to cook or clean house.
    I'm not going to do any work.   I'm going to have a good rest.

They don't like this house; they're going to look for somewhere else to live.

B   We **don't** use **GOING TO** for fixed plans:
I've got my ticket; I'm taking the train to Manchester at 3.45 pm.
For fixed plans see Unit 21

We **don't** use **GOING TO** when somebody else tells us what to do:
"Can you type this letter for me?"
"Yes, I'll do it this afternoon."

FORM

Affirmative	**Negative**	**Interrogative**
She is going to see Robert.	She is not going to see Robert.	Is she going to see Robert?

For contractions see Unit 1

Good English?

② Look at the <u>underlined</u> parts of these sentences. Two of them are correct and two are wrong.
Tick (✔) the correct ones, and rewrite the wrong ones.

.... 1   He's <u>going to</u> play football on Saturday.   3   You <u>going to</u> see that film?
.... 2   I <u>don't going to</u> see them next week.   4   <u>Is</u> she <u>going to</u> stay with her uncle?

Two Young People Who Know What They Want

③ Robert and Carol talk to their Auntie Mabel abut what they want to do in the future. Complete the gaps in their stories with suitable forms of GOING TO.

Robert

1 *Mabel* Well, Robert, you're 24 now; what .... (you) do next?

2 *Robert* I .... stay in my present job for a few years, but remember, Auntie, next year I .... get married!

3 *Mabel* Where .... (you) live?

4 *Robert* We .... stay in Hampton, because I want to be near my parents. We .... rent a small flat.

5 *Mabel* You can't have children in a small flat!

6 *Robert* Don't worry, we .... (not) have children immediately. We .... wait for two or three years.

Carol

7 *Mabel* Carol what .... (you) do when you finish university?

8 *Carol* I .... travel for six months. Then I .... come back to England, and I .... get a job.

9 *Mabel* What .... (you) do when you come back?

10 *Carol* Well, I .... (not) be a secretary, and I .... (not) be a housewife.

11 *Mabel* OK, you told me what you .... (not) do; what .... (you) do?

12 *Carol* I .... be a fashion model.

13 *Mabel* (laughing) Oh yes, and I .... be a film star!

What Is the Company Going To Do?

④ Using GOING TO, expand these notes to make sentences.

Example: *We are going to expand our line of software products.* .... (expand)

1 .... (new factory)
2 .... (more staff)
3 .... (new machines)
4 .... (new markets)

It's a Mad, Mad World!

⑤ Complete this dialogue with appropriate forms of GOING TO.

Isabella What .... (you) going to do now, Christopher?

Columbus I .... sail to America!

Isabella What's that?

Columbus It's a new continent. I .... discover it.

Isabella And why .... (you) call it America?

Columbus Because it's full of Americans!

(Note: Columbus thought he was in India.
America was called America in 1507, after Amerigo Vespucci.)

I'LL DO IT (future - 3)

Look at these pictures, and study the texts.

*"In five years' time,
you will be eighteen."*

"I am going to Moscow in January."
"It will be cold there."

① Complete these sentences in the same way, using a verb from the box for each sentence.

elect   be   go

1   In two years Peter .... to university.
2   "I'm going to West Africa"
     "It .... hot there."
3   The country .... a new president in the year 2002.

USE

We use **WILL** for talking abut the future, especially when we are sure something is true:

     We will start the new millenium in the year 2001.
         (We are sure this is true.)
     Jane will go to university when she is 18.
         (I am reasonably sure this is true; it is very probable.)
     "The concert will begin in five minutes' time."
         (The announcer is sure this is true.)
     "It'll be cold in Moscow in December."
         (The speaker is sure.)

FORM

Affirmative   I **will** be here.
Negative   She **will not** be here. (**She won't** be here.)
Interrogative   **Will you** be here?

We normally use **will** (or usually **'ll**) for the future.
We usually use **'ll** with "I", but we can use **shall** or **will**:
         I'll (shall/will) be here at 8.15.

(Note: We often use **shall** for offers:
         It's hot in here. **Shall I** open the window?)

I'LL DO IT (future - 3)

Good English?

② Look at the <u>underlined</u> parts in these sentences. Two of them are correct and two are wrong. Tick (✔) the correct ones, and rewrite the wrong ones.

...............1   <u>You will</u> be here tomorrow? 3   I <u>will tell</u> him tomorrow.
...............2   They <u>won't like</u> the idea! 4   John and Peter <u>not will go</u> to Paris.

What Do You Think Will Happen?

③ Complete these sentences with WILL or WON'T according to your opinion.

1   I .... fly to Beijing tomorrow.
2   Next year, I .... be one year older.
3   The Queen of England .... open many exhibitions this year.
4   Robert .... become a concert pianist; he's too old.

④ Now complete these sentences, using expressions from the box and WILL or WON'T, as in the example.

| I don't think   I think   I'm sure |

Example: *I'm sure I won't get married this year.*

5   .... do well in my next examination.
6   .... compete in the Olympic Games
7   .... learn to speak English one day.
8   .... I'll make a lot of money soon.

What Will the Weather Be Like?

⑤ Look at this weather chart for today.

Wales	Scotland	England	London	Paris
rain	snow	be cloudy	be foggy	be sunny

Four drivers and a waiter are discussing the weather for today. A tourist is listening.
Complete the sentences.

1 *Driver 1*   I'm driving to Scotland.
   Waiter   .... there.
2 *Driver 2*   I'm going to London.
   Waiter   .... there.
3 *Driver 3*   I'm heading for Central England.
   Waiter   .... there.
4 *Driver 4*   I'm driving to Wales.
   Waiter   .... there.
5 *Tourist*   Well, I'm going to Paris.
               .... there!

STOP NO STOPPING BE CAREFUL   (imperatives)

Here are the orders given in ROAD SIGNS.

A   B   C

Turn left   No cycling   Overtaking prohibited

① Here are five road signs like the one in A. Write the correct phrase from the box in next to each sign (two are easy!).

Turn right	Give way	
Stop	Pass either side	Keep left

1 ....   2 ....   3 ....

4 ....   5 ....

② Here are five road signs like the one in B. Write the correct phrase from the box in next to each sign.

No entry	No right turn	No stopping
No pedestrians		No U turns

1 ....   2 ....   3 ....

4 ....   5 ....

③ Here are three road signs like the one in C. Write the correct phrase from the box in next to each sign.

All motor vehicles prohibited	Vehicles over
7.5 tons prohibited	All vehicles prohibited

1 ....   2 ....   3 ....

USE

We use these pictures and expressions on ROAD SIGNS, and in MANUALS FOR DRIVERS, but not when we speak.

Writing:	*Speaking:*
No entry	"You musn't drive in there."
	OR "Don't drive in there."
Turn left	"You've got to turn left."
All vehicles prohibited	"Vehicles aren't allowed in there."

Now look at this picture, and study the text.

"It's a lovely day;
let's not stay indoors;
let's go for a walk!"

USE

We use **LET'S** (let us) and **LET'S NOT** (affirmative) to make suggestions:
     Let's have a game of football.
     Let's not go out tonight; I want to watch TV.
There are two negative forms:
     Let's not go out.
     Don't let's go out.

Explaining Road Signs

④ You have to explain these road signs to someone who does not understand them, as in the example.

Example: What does this sign mean?

It means ...*you've got to stop.*...... [STOP]

   1   What does this sign mean?
It means ....

   2   What does this sign mean?
It means ....

GIVE WAY   3   What does this sign mean?
It means ....

   4   What does this sign mean?
It means ....

Suggestions

⑤ Now you have to rewrite the sentences, using LET'S or LET'S NOT.

1   You don't want to go out to supper tonight.
"..."

2   You would like to go the cinema with the girls.
"..."

3   You want to suggest a visit to the theatre for everybody.
"..."

4   You don't want to go to see Auntie Mabel this evening.

"..."

MIXED EXERCISES   (all tense units)

Here are four exercises which use all the tenses presented in this section. Note that in these exercises, there is sometimes more than one way to fill a blank. A different verb tense usually changes the meaning of a sentence.

Present simple: He walks   *Past simple:*   He walked
   continuous: He is walking   *continuous:*   He was walking
Present perfect: He has walked
Future: 1 He is walking 2 He will walk 3 He is going to walk

① Read these four passages, and put the verbs in the brackets in the correct tense.

A   It is 7 o'clock in the evening. Robert and Carol are in Robert's car; they .... (drive) to his office. Robert .... (not take) his car to the office every day; he .... (usually, go) by train. And he .... (not, usually, go) to the office in the evening.

B   But today is a special day. The office manager .... (give) a party, and he .... (ask) Robert to bring his sister. Robert .... (wear) slacks. He .... (not, usually, wear) slacks to the office; he .... (usually, wear) a dark suit.

C   Robert .... (speak) to Carol last week and .... (ask) her if she wanted to go to the party. She .... (say) yes, because she wants to see Robert's office.

D   This evening Carol is dressed up too: she .... (wear) a party dress and high heels. She .... (not, know) anybody in Robert's office; perhaps she .... (meet) somebody she likes!

② Put in the correct tense of the verbs in the brackets in each of these sentences.

1   "What .... (you, read)?" "It's a book by Barbara Cartland."
2   Dennis Johnston .... (work) for an insurance company.
3   Be careful with that glass; you .... (break) it!
4   "............. (you, take) your medicine yet?"
5   They .... (leave) the house when Jimmy ran in.
6   I .... (wake) up at 6 am yesterday morning.
7   Carol .... (stay) with her grandmother this week.
8   She .... (not, buy) the coat; it was too expensive.
9   He's very hardworking; I think he .... (do) the job well.
10   Dennis .... (not, like) his work much.
11   At what time .... (the play, begin) last night?
12   "I .... (read) this novel last night, but couldn't finish it."
13   I .... (hear) that piece of music many times before.
14   "............. (you, have) supper when I phoned?"
15   "What .... (you, do) tonight" "I haven't got any plans."
16   Uncle Victor .... (not, work) today. He's tired.
17   "............. (you, play) the piano?" "No, I don't."
18   My plane .... (leave) at 7.45 tomorrow morning.
19   "Let's go." "Wait a minute, I .... (not, pay) the bill."
20   What clothes .... (you, take) with you to Moscow?"

③ Read these four passages, and put the verbs in brackets in the correct tense.

A   ".............. (you, see) the new film at the Odeon yet?"
    "Yes, we have."
    "When .... (you, go)?"
    "We .... (go) last night at seven o'clock."
    "............. (you, enjoy) it?"
    "Yes, we did. I .... (not, see) a film like that for a long time."

B   "............. (you, speak) to John recently?"
    "No, I .... (see) him tomorrow."
    "Where .... (he, live) these days?"
    "I'm not sure. He .... (live) in Hampstead, but I think he .... (move) house last
    month. Now he .... (live) in Camden, I think."
    "And where .... (he, work) now?"
    "I .... (not, know)."

C   "Carol, when .... (you see) Steven next?"
    "Well, yesterday an old friend of mine .... (give) me two tickets for the musical 'Cats', so
    Steven and .... (see) that together tomorrow night. Why did you ask, Mum?"
    "I .... (want) you to ask him round for dinner on Saturday. I .... (have) several
    people for dinner"
    "Oh dear!"

D   "Robert, can you help me with my homework?"
    "What subject is it?"
    "Algebra."
    "Well, I .... (help) you if I can, but when I was at school I .... (not, understand)
    algebra at all. But I .... (try) to help you. When .... (the teacher, collect) the
    homework?"
    "She .... (say) Monday, but she .... probably .... (forget). She often ....
    (forget) to collect our homework."

④ Put the verbs given in the correct tenses.

1   Mr Baker .... (come) home at 6 pm last night.
2   .... you .... (talk) to your boss about a raise?
3   I .... (finish) this job next week.
4   I .... (not, take) John to school yesterday because he wasn't well.
5   Let's go. .... Peter .... (come) with us?
6   I don't want to see that film again. I .... (see) it twice already!
7   "Where is Mike?" "He .... (stay) with his grandmother this weekend."
8   I .... (not, like) peanut butter!
9   Last week he .... (sell) his car and .... (buy) a new one.
10 "What .... John .... (do) when you got home?" "He was lying on the couch
    watching the telly!"
11 Fred .... (finish) his homework and now he is playing in the garden.
12 "............. you .... (see) that programme on Turkey last night? It was wonderful."
13 Planes .... (take) off and .... (land) at Heathrow all day.
14 "What time .... your plane .... (leave)?" "At 7.45."
15 Uncle Victor is 88 years old. He .... (see) everything and .... (do) everything.

I WILL   I MAY   I WON'T (probability)

Look at these pictures, and study the texts.

Robert will finish at six.

Dennis may finish at six.

Fred won't finish at six.

① Now complete these sentences in the same way.

1   Susan .... marry Robert, because she doesn't like him.
2   Fred .... watch TV this evening; he always does.
3   Carol .... get the job as secretary; she isn't sure.

USE		
Affirmative	**Negative**	**Interrogative**
will....	He won't....	Will you?....
won't = will not		

FORM	
A WILL. YES. *It is certain/definite.* Tom will have something to eat today. I will go to work/school next week.	B MAY. *It is possible.* She may change to a different job next year. They may buy a new house.
C WON'T. NO. *Definitely not.* You won't live for a thousand years. He won't win the race; he's too fat.	

Good English?

② Look at the <u>underlined</u> parts of these sentences. Three of them are correct, and three are wrong.
Tick (✓) the correct ones, and rewrite the wrong ones.

.... 1   <u>Will you come</u> tomorrow?
.... 2   <u>I don't may have</u> time.
.... 3   <u>She not will do</u> it.
.... 4   <u>They will not catch</u> the plane.
.... 5   <u>Do you will help</u> me?
.... 6   <u>He may win</u> the match; I'm not sure.

The Johnsons and Mr Mad

③ Here are four people, with different characters. What will they do today? Look at the chart. Now complete these sentences.

		ROBERT	CAROL	VICTORIA	MR MAD
(a)	get to work/school on time	✓	?	✓	✗
(b)	be late for work/school	✗	?	✗	✓
(c)	help Carol with her homework	?	-	✓	✗
(d)	forget to have lunch	✗	✗	✗	✗
(e)	enjoy the concert on Saturday	?	✓	✓	✗

1 (a) Victoria .... get to work on time. (b) She .... be late for work.
   (c) She .... help Carol with her homework. (d) She .... forget to have lunch.
   (e) She .... enjoy the concert on Saturday.

2 (a) Robert .... on time. (b) He .... work.
   (c) He .... homework. (d) He .... lunch.
   (e) He .... Saturday.

3 (a) Carol .... on time. (b) She .... school.
   (c) She .... lunch. (d) She .... Saturday.

4 (a) Mr Mad .... on time. (b) He .... work.
   (c) He .... homework. (d) He .... lunch.
   (e) He .... Saturday.

THE FUTURE: What Will Happen To You? Is It Certain or Not?

④ Think about these possible events in your country and your life. In your opinion, are they "WILL" events, "MAY" events or "WON'T" events? Where possible complete each sentence more than once.

In Your Country
   1 There .... an election tomorrow/next year/in five years .
   2 It .... be cold next June/September/December.
   3 There .... be a lot of rain/snow/where I live/next week/month.
   4 The authorities .... build a new stadium/park/museum.

On Your Life
   1 Next year we .... be older/younger/fatter/thinner.
   2 I .... have my hair cut this afternoon/this week/this month/this year.
   3 I .... get married tomorrow/this year/one day.
   4 I .... learn English tomorrow/this year/one day.
   5 I .... be a famous pianist/lawyer/architect/business man one day.

I CAN   I CANNOT   (ability)

Look at these pictures. and study the texts.

Carol can swim well.   *Robert can swim a little.*   *Fred cannot swim.*

*When she was six,
Carol could swim.*

*When he was nine,
Robert couldn't swim.*

① Now look at these pictures, and complete the sentences with words from the box.

can	well
cannot	a little

1   Mary .... cook.
2   Brian .... cook ....
3   Sarah .... cook ....

And finally complete these sentences.

4   When he was 15, Brian .... cook; he learnt when he was 18.
5   When Sarah was 10, she .... cook a little; her mother taught her when she
    was very young.

USE

Ability

We use **CAN** in the present and **COULD** in the past:

> He can speak French.
>
> Years ago, most people could ride a horse; today, they can't.

We use **CAN/COULD** frequently with these verbs:

> see hear smell understand remember

Examples: I can hear music!

> They couldn't understand what I said.

Writing (usually):   cannot   could not

Speaking (usually):   can't   couldn't   For **CAN** (permission and requests) see also Unit 29

Good English?

② Look at the <u>underlined</u> parts of these sentences. Four of them are correct and three are wrong. Tick (✓) the correct ones, and rewrite the wrong ones.

............1   I <u>can't understand</u> what you're saying.
............2   Years ago, he <u>could play</u> tennis well.
............3   I <u>not can do</u> this.
............4   He <u>didn't could</u> come.
............5   It was late, and he <u>couldn't wait</u>.
............6   Last year Carol <u>can't speak</u> Russian, but now she can.
............7   <u>Could you speak</u> French before you went to Paris?

Two Secretaries

③ Here are two candidates for a post as secretary to the General Manager of JUNK Foods Ltd. Last year they were not good secretaries, but they have taken training.

		JOSEPH		KATHLEEN		KEY
		Last year	This year	Last year	This year	✓✓✓ = Very well
1	type	✗	✓	✓	✓	✓✓ = well
2	use a word processor	✓	✓✓	✗	✓✓	✓ = (not) very well
3	keep accounts	✗	✗	✗	✗	✗ = (not)
4	take dictation	✗	✓	✗	✗	
5	use an audio machine	✓	✓✓✓	✗	✓	

Look at the tables and the key, then complete the sentences below.

1   Joseph .... type last year, but this year he .... type ....
2   Kathleen .... use a word processor .... this year, but last year she .... use a word processor.
3   Joseph .... keep accounts last year, and he .... keep accounts this year!
4   Kathleen .... type .... last year, and this year she .... type ....
5   Joseph .... use a word processor .... last year, but this year he .... use one ....
6   Kathleen .... take dictation last year, and this year she .... either!
7   Joseph .... use an audio machine .... , but this year he .... use one ....
8   Kathleen .... keep accounts last year, and she .... keep accounts this year!

You and Your Family

④ Write five sentences about you/your family, like this:
   ...*I can ride a horse.*.........................

Use: I   play the piano/video/guitar/football/tennis/golf
       my brother/sister   ride a bicycle/horse
       my father/grandfather   drive a car/lorry/tractor
       my cousin etc.   run 100 metres in 10 seconds

HAVE TO   MUSTN'T   DON'T HAVE TO
(obligation in present and past)

Look at these pictures, and study the texts.

"Oh, do you have to leave so soon?"
"Yes, I have to go home."

"Where's Carol?"
"She had to go home."
"Oh, why did she have to go home?"

① Now complete these sentences with words from the box, in affirmative or interrogative.

have to   had to

1   Jimmy .... finish his supper before he could watch TV.
2   .... we .... wait, or can we go?
3   They .... stay at school for two hours yesterday evening.
4   "............. you .... dance with that horrible man?"

Now look at these pictures, and study the texts.

"You mustn't do that;
it's very naughty!"

"You don't have to finish that today, and you didn't have
to come so early in the morning - still it was very kind of you!"

② And finally complete these sentences with words from the box.

| mustn't   doesn't have to |
didn't have to

1   Admission was free, so they .... pay.
2   You .... cross the road without looking.
3   He is well off, so he .... work for a living.

USE

Notice the difference between prohibition; obligation and no obligation:

	PROHIBITION	OBLIGATION	NO OBLIGATION
Present	You mustn't	You have to/must	You don't have to
Past		You had	You didn't have to

Good English?

③ Look at the underlined parts of these sentences. Three of them are correct and three are wrong. Tick (✓) the correct ones, and rewrite the wrong ones.

..............1 He didn't have to go to Manchester last week.
..............2 You don't must wait here.
..............3 Anyone can go to a shop, but you mustn't buy anything.
..............4 You must breathe to live.
..............5 He had to catch the 6.35 train.
..............6 They can't go today. They have wait till tomorrow.

More Practice

④ Complete these sentences with the right tense of HAVE TO.

1 Carol wasn't feeling well, so she .... go home.
2 We .... go or we'll miss the 8.33 train.
3 Uncle Victor hasn't come, so we .... do all his work.
4 You .... wait for the traffic to stop before you cross the street.
5 Ophelia .... stay in her bowl all the time.
6 Jimmy couldn't mend his bicycle, so he .... take it to the bicycle repair shop.

⑤ Complete these sentences with DO/DID YOU HAVE TO?

Example:
"In my office, everybody wears a suit and a tie."
"Why ..... *do* ..... (you) ..... *have to wear a suit and tie* .?"

1 "I had to pay the community charge last week."
   "Oh dear. How much....................................?"
2 "Robert has to write reports for his boss."
   "How often...?"
3 "Last week I had to get up early every day."
   "Why...?"
4 "I'm leaving for Siberia next Tuesday."
   "Why...?"

⑥ Complete these sentences with the right tense of MUSTN'T, HAVE TO or DON'T/DIDN'T HAVE TO.

Example:
It was Sunday yesterday, so we stayed in bed. We ..... *didn't have to get up* ..... early.

1 You have to be quiet in the library; you .... talk.
2 When you go to a picture gallery, you .... touch the pictures, but you .... look at them if you don't want to.
3 The concert was free, so we .... pay.
4 Carol's friend Elizabeth Taylor has got plenty of money; she .... work.
5 "............. you .... take your driving test more than once?"
6 "Yes, I .... take it three times. But I .... take the eye test three times; I only .... take that once."

CAN (asking for and giving permission)
WOULD YOU LIKE (making and accepting offers)

First look at these pictures, and study the texts which show examples of asking for and giving permission.

"Can we come in?"
"No, I'm sorry, you can't."

"Can I come in?"
"Yes, certainly, you can.

① Now complete these dialogues.

1 "............. a table for two, please?"
2 "............. sir, ... , we are full."
3 "............. for three, please?"
4 "............. Lord Elgin, we have a table over here."

Look at these pictures, and study the texts which show examples of making and accepting offers.

"Would you like to have dinner tonight?"
"Yes, I'd like to, thank you very much."

"Would you like to come to the cinema tonight?"
"No, sorry, I'm afraid I can't."

② Now complete these dialogues.

1 "................................... to a concert tonight?"
   "Yes .... , ..."
2 "................................. to the pub for a drink?"
   "No ...., ..."

USE
PERMISSION and response
We use **CAN:**   Can I come in? Yes, certainly.
No, I'm sorry, you can't.
OFFERS and response
We use **WOULD YOU LIKE:**   Would you like a cup of tea? Yes, I'd like one.
No thank you.

Good English?

③ Read these three dialogues. In each case *either* the permission/offer is wrong *or* the response is wrong. Tick (✓) the correct ones, and rewrite the wrong ones.

.............1 a <u>Can you</u> help me?
....   b <u>No, I'm sorry,</u> how can I help?
.............2 a <u>Would I like</u> to sit down?
....   b <u>No, I'm sorry,</u> that seat's taken.

.............3 a <u>Would you like</u> a cup of tea?
....   b <u>Yes, certainly,</u> I'll make one.

More Practice

④ Complete these questions and answers with words from the box

can I	I'm sorry
you	certainly

Questions
1 .... ask you a question?
2 .... tell me the time, please?
3 .... wait a moment?
4 .... sit next to you?

Answers
A No, ... , this seat's taken.
B Yes, ... , what do you want to know?
C No, ... , I'm in a hurry.
D Yes, ... , it's five past six.

⑤ Complete the missing parts of this conversation in your own words, using the new phrases in this unit.

A .... for supper this evening?
B Oh, that's very kind of you. What time .... ?
A Oh, about seven or seven thirty will be fine.
B .... my wife with me?
A I didn't know she was here. .... , we .... to see her.
B .... us to bring anything? A bottle of wine?
A No, nothing at all, but thank you anyway.

Normal or Strange?

⑥ Read these dialogues; which picture do they belong to?

1 "Water!"
   "Here, drink this and shut up."
   "Glug!"

2 "Can I have a glass of water, please?"
   "Yes, certainly. Would you like fizzy or still?"
   "Still, please. Thank you very much."

Now read the dialogues again, and make up polite dialogues, using the same information.

3 "Give me a ride!"
   "Get in!"
   "Aaaaah!"

4 "A seat!"
   "Sit there!"
   "Uff!"

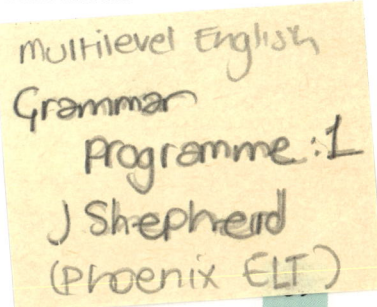

Multilevel English
Grammar
Programme: 1
J Shepherd
(Phoenix ELT)

MIXED EXERCISES (units 26 - 29)

Here are four exercises which use all the modals practised in Units 26-29.

probability	**ability**	**obligation**
He will	You can	He has to
I may	I cannot (can't)	You mustn't
You won't	She could	We don't have to
	They couldn't	

requests and responses	**invitations and responses**
Can I?	Would you like to?
certainly	I'd like to
I'm sorry	I'm afraid I can't

Mixed Bag - 1

① Complete each sentence with one of the two words or phrases given at the end of the sentence.

1	You .... cross the road here; it's not safe!	CAN/MUSTN'T
2	Robert .... get married next year; he's not sure.	CAN'T/MAY
	Fred .... get married next year; he's too young!	WON'T/WILL
3	Would .... come to dinner with me tonight?	COULD/YOU LIKE TO
	Thank you, ... very much.	I'D LIKE TO/I'M AFRAID
4	Fred .... drive a car; he's only twelve.	CAN'T/COULDN'T
	Robert .... drive,	COULD/CAN
	but he .... drive when he was twelve.	CAN'T/COULDN'T
5	.... watch television, Robert?	CAN I/WILL I
	No, ... Fred,	CERTAINLY/I'M SORRY
	you .... finish your homework first.	MAY/HAVE TO
6	.... you like another piece of cake?	DO/WOULD
	.... I can't; I'm watching my weight.	I'M AFRAID/CERTAINLY
	But you're very slim!	
	You .... worry about your weight!	CAN'T/DON'T HAVE TO

Mixed Bag - 2

② Match each of these phrases with the most appropriate phrase alongside. Look at *all* the phrases before deciding.

1	It will rain	A	all day and all night forever!
2	It may rain	B	on the day of my open-air picnic!
3	It won't rain	C	at least once this year.
4	It mustn't rain	D	next month.

1	Can I sit here?	A	Yes, I'd like that.
2	Would you like to join me for lunch today?	B	Yes, certainly, help yourself.
3	Can I have an apple?	C	I'm afraid I can't today.
4	Would you like lunch next week?	D	No, I'm sorry, this seat's taken.

A New Trainee Arrives At the Montessori School In Italy

③ Jane is an old student. She is explaining to Chris, who is a new student, about the lectures and the language of the school. Complete the sentences with words or phrases at the top of the previous page.

Jane	Welcome to the school! I'm sure you'll have a good time if you work hard. You .... arrive early for lectures during the week. You .... attend lectures on Sundays. You .... be late for lectures, and you .... get up early from Monday to Friday, but on Saturday you .... get up early if you don't want to. All the lectures are in Italian. .... you speak Italian?
Chris	Two years I .... speak Italian at all, but now I .... understand quite well, but I .... speak much.
Jane	Well, you .... learn as quickly as you can! .... you take extra Italian classes?
Chris	Yes, ... I think I .... learn quickly, because everyone speaks Italian here.
Jane	Yes, that's right. Now, ... go and see the cafeteria?
Chris	Oh, yes! Anne .... we have a cup of coffee?
Jane	No, ... It's closed until eleven o'clock.
Chris	But it's eleven o'clock now. .... a cup of coffee? I'll invite you!
Jane	Yes, ... , thank you very much!

A Young Woman At University Talks To Her Tutor

④ Here is a conversation between Susan, a young university student, and her tutor, Mr Briggs. You have to complete the conversation with appropriate words or phrases:

Susan	Good morning, Mr Briggs, ... come and see you tomorrow?
Briggs	No, tomorrow I .... be here. But you .... see me now if you like. .... to sit down?
Susan	Oh, thank you. But I haven't got much time, because I .... finish the book you lent me last week.
Briggs	Oh, don't worry, you .... finish it next week. Have you written your essay?
Susan	.... Mr Briggs, ... I haven't. But I .... give it to you next Monday, I promise.
Briggs	What's today, Friday. Well, you .... give it to me on Monday, but you .... give it to me by next Friday. That's the last day.
Susan	Don't worry, Mr Briggs. I .... finish it by Friday.
Briggs	.... to come and have tea with my wife and I on Saturday?
Susan	.... , I'm playing tennis in the college team on Saturday.
Briggs	.... come on Sunday, then?
Susan	Oh yes, ... , thank you very much.
Briggs	You .... wear formal clothes; we're very informal on the weekend.
Susan	I .... there about four; is that all right?
Briggs	You .... be there at four. Five o'clock is fine. .... bring your boyfriend with you?
Susan	Well, ... I haven't got a boyfriend at present.

IT IS MADE (the passive)

Look at these pictures, and study the texts.

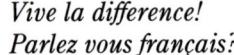

Vive la différence!
Parlez vous français?

French is spoken in Paris.

These cars were made in Germany.

① Now complete these sentences with the right form of SPEAK or MAKE and IS/ARE/WAS/WERE.

1   English and Spanish .... in many countries.
2   The first bicycle .... in Scotland in 1839.
3   Latin .... in Italy 2,000 years ago.
4   Beer .... in many countries.

FORM

The Passive
Simple Present:
    People speak French in Quebec.
              French is spoken in Quebec.
Simple Past:
    Someone made this car in Germany.
              This car was made in Germany.

	Affirmative	**Negative**	**Interrogative**
Present	Beer is made.	Beer is not made.	Is beer made?
Past	Horses were used.	Horses were not used.	Were horses used?

Writing (usually): are not   was not
Speaking (usually): aren't   wasn't

See Unit 19 Form
Also: drink   drank   drunk
        sell   sold   sold
        steal   stole   stolen

Good English?

② Look at the <u>underlined</u> parts of these sentences. Three of them are correct and three are wrong.
Tick (✓) the correct ones, and rewrite the wrong ones.

.... 1   <u>Volkswagens are made</u> in Brazil today.
.... 2   This car <u>didn't was made</u> in Germany.
.... 3   Poor <u>Sally was bitten</u> by a dog!
.... 4   <u>Champagne is produce</u> in France.
.... 5   <u>Was born Carol</u> in London?
.... 6   <u>Are cars made</u> of steel or plastic? (Both!)

Forming the Passive

③ Complete each sentence with a passive form of the verb, present or past.

1 All trains .... yesterday because of a security alert. (cancel)
2 He was .... of a terrible crime. (accuse)
3 The first goal .... by Maradona. (score)
4 The sheets .... once a month. (change)
5 Telephones .... by Alexander Bell. (invent)
6 Most of our cars .... to other countries. (export)
7 St Paul's Cathedral .... about the year 1700. (build)
8 "When .... your car .... , sir?" (steal)
9 Wine is often .... with dinner in Spain. (serve)
10 Sentences can be .... in the active or the passive. (write)

Writing and Rewriting the Passive

④ Now you have to rewrite these active sentences, so that they have the same meaning in the passive.

1 They translated the treaty into four languages.
The treaty ....
2 People don't use these books much.
These books..
3 Last year they built a new motorway in Kent.
A new motorway..
4 How often do they change the restaurant menu?
How often is...?
5 They sell stamps here.
Stamps...
6 Handel wrote "The Messiah" in six weeks.
"The Messiah"..
7 Do people borrow many books from the library?
Are many...?
8 They don't sell books in supermarkets in England.
Books..

⑤ Now you have to make up sentences in the passive, using the words given.

1 The date of the meeting/change/at the last minute
....
2 Robert/attack and rob/in the street
....
3 The shopping centre/finish/last year
....
4 Buses/use/every day by thousands of people
....
5 Service/include/bill
....
6 The streets/clean/once a week
....

GET GO (phrasal verbs –1)

Read this text, and think abut the words in **bold**.

In the morning Jimmy and Robert **get up** at about 7 o'clock. Robert **goes in** the bathroom first. Later they go downstairs, make their breakfast and **go out**. Outside, Robert **gets in** his car and goes to the office, and Jimmy **gets on** his bicycle and goes to school.

At the office, Robert **gets out** of his car and goes to the lift. He **goes up** to the 7th floor. Later he **goes down** to the 6th floor to see his boss.

At school, Jimmy **gets off** his bicycle and **goes in** the school building.

Now look at these pictures, and the verbs with each picture.

"EASY"

"DIFFICULT"

① Complete these sentences with GO, GET in the past tense and a preposition, IN, OUT, ON, OFF, DOWN or THROUGH.

1   Peter .... at 7am and .... the bathroom.
2   The man .... the bus near his house and .... at the office.
3   .... the front door, ... the stairs to the 2nd floor.
4   She .... the underground station, ... the escalator and .... the train.

Good English?

② Look at the <u>underlined</u> parts of these sentences. Four of them are correct and four are wrong.
  Tick (✓) the correct ones, and rewrite the wrong ones.

...............1   If it rains, they'll <u>go in</u> the house.
...............2   Uncle Victor <u>got up</u> his car and left.
...............3   I <u>get up</u> every day at 6.00 am.
...............4   You can <u>go off</u> the bus at the next stop.
...............5   "<u>Get down</u> your bicycle, Jimmy!"
...............6   When you <u>go in</u> the museum, rent the taped commentary.
...............7   <u>Go down</u> the stairs and wait for me in the hall.
...............8   "<u>Get in</u> the living room and sit down somewhere."

Easy or Difficult?

③ Complete these pictures by writing the correct phrases in each box. One has been done for you.

GET	GO
get up	go up
get down	go down
get in	go in
get out	go out
get on	
get off	

④ Now complete these sentences with the verbs in these five boxes (some alternatives are possible).

> go down   go in
> get in

1   In her university holidays, Carol works as a "temp". Her office is on the second floor. At lunchtime she .... the lift and .... to the ground floor. Then she .... the cafeteria and has lunch.

> get out   go in
> get in   go out

2   At five o'clock she finishes work. She .... of the building, ... her car, and drives home. At home she............ of her car and .... the house.

> get off   get on

3   Sometimes she walks to work; then in the evening she .... the 47 bus near the corner of her office, and .... near her house.

> go in   go up
> get up

4   Before supper she usually .... to her bedroom on the first floor and changes her clothes. After supper she .... the living room and watches TV for an hour. Carol usually goes to bed abut 10.30, and .... at six.

> get on   get off

5   Yesterday Fred .... the table and stood there. "............!" his sister Carol shouted, but Fred just laughed.

PUT   TAKE (phrasal verbs – 2)

Look at these pictures, and study the texts.

Take that sweater off.

Put this coat on.

Take everything out of your pockets, please

Put everything back, except the gun

USE

A   In the pictures above, we give four movements.

B   Here are some other uses:
   Put the light on (also: switch on, turn on).
   Put the light off (also: switch off, turn off).
   She turned the television on.
   The prices went up last month.
   His temperature went down after taking aspirins.
   Her grades have gone up this year.

FORM

Here we have eight prepositions (particles):

up	down	in	out	on	off	back	away

Notice the word order:

VERB	(OBJECT)	PREPOSITION
come		in
go		away
put	this coat	on

Good English?

① Four of these prepositions are correct and three are wrong. The wrong ones may be a) the wrong preposition, or b) the wrong position. Tick (✓) the correct ones, and rewrite the wrong ones.

.... 1   Put the light <u>in</u> please; it's dark <u>in</u> here.

.... 2   He put his coat <u>on</u> when he went <u>off</u>.

.... 3   When he came <u>back</u>, he took <u>off</u> it.

.... 4   He said goodbye and walked <u>in</u>.

Putting Together Phrasal Verbs

② Complete each sentence with the best preposition from the box.

on	off	in	out
up	back	away	

1   Hello, John. Come .... !
2   It's warm here; I'll take my pullover ....
3   The price of coal is going .... this winter, I'm afraid.
4   When you've washed the cups, put them .... in their place.
5   The cat's in the cupboard, and she won't come ....
6   "Where is your son?" "He's gone .... for six months, to see the world."
7   Put your raincoat .... ; it's raining outside.

③ Complete each sentence with the correct form of one of the phrasal verbs given in the box.

put away	come back
go in	take out

1   When the bell rings, ... the meat .... of the oven.
2   He finished his work and .... his books ....
3   Can you .... my office and wait for me there?
4   She left at one o'clock and .... at three.

put down	go out
come down	take away

5   "Fred! It's 8 o'clock;   .... and eat your breakfast!"
6   She put on her coat and .... for a walk.
7   "............. that suitcase .... and open the door."
8   He picked up the rubbish and .... it ....

④ Complete each sentence with a verb from one box and a preposition from the other box.

go	come
take	go

away	down
up	out

1   "Let's take the car and .... for a drive."
2   "How is the patient?" "Worse, doctor. His temperature .... last night."
3   Where's Peter?"
    "Upstairs."
    "Ask him to .... and help me."
4   "Can you .... those old magazines .... and throw them in the bin?"

put	come
put	take

back	out
down	off

5   When you have finished with the scissors, please .... them .... in the drawer.
6   Men usually .... their hats .... in a church.
7   "The sun is shining; .... into the garden!"
8   "Can you .... the box .... on the floor, please?"

MIXED EXERCISES (units 32 – 33)

GET	GO	COME	PUT	TAKE
get up	go up	come up	put on	take down
get down	go down	come down	put off (switch)	take out
get in	go in	come in	put back	take off
get out	go out	come off	put away	take away
get on	go back	come back		
get off	go away			

Mixed Bag

① Complete each blank with one of the phrasal verbs in the box above. (Sometimes the two words are together, and sometimes they are separated.)

1 Mr Simpson .... the taxi outside his house, and .... at the opera house.

2 Peter .... his bike outside his house, and .... at the cinema.

3 The young man .... to Australia, where he stayed for a long time, but 20 years later he .... to his old home.

4 I knocked on the door of the office. "............. !" said a voice, so I opened the door and ....

5 He .... his passport .... of his pocket, and showed it to the immigration officer.

6 John .... his clothes and went to bed.

7 "Waiter, we don't want this ashtray. Will you please .... it .... the table."

8 "John, where are you?"
"I'm upstairs."
"Can you .... and help me?"

9 With great difficulty, the climbers .... the mountain and arrived at the bottom.

10 "This old armchair is horrible. Can you ask someone to .... it .... ?"

11 "I don't like those pictures on the wall. Let's .... them .... and .... them .... in a cupboard."

Up a Tree

② Complete each blank with one of the phrasal verbs in the box above.

1 Fred .... his bicycle and cycled to his friend's house.
When he arrived, he .... his bicycle.

2 Fred's friend was up a tree in the garden, and his mother .... of her house and shouted: "Willy! .... now, you'll hurt yourself."

3 But his friend didn't move, so his mother .... in the house. Willy said, "Do you want to .... here with me?" So Fred .... the tree too.

4 It was easy to .... , but it was more difficult to .... down.

Carol Cleans Her Room

③ Complete each blank with one of the phrasal verbs from the box on the previous page.

1 Carol never cleans her room, but yesterday morning very early, she decided it was time.

2 She .... at six am. It was still dark, so she .... the light. Then she .... the bathroom, had a shower, and .... some old clothes.

3 Then she .... to the kitchen, ... the kettle .... , and made herself a strong cup of coffee.

4 Then she .... to her room, and .... all her sweaters .... of the drawer and .... them .... the bed. She folded them carefully, and .... them .... in the drawer.

5 Then she opened the next drawer. She found a lot of old clothes, so she decided to .... them .... a suitcase.

6 There was a big suitcase on top of the cupboard. She .... a chair, ... the suitcase .... , and .... the old clothes .... it.

7 Fred heard the noise, and .... to see what she was doing, but he soon .... again. He wasn't interested!

8 But five minutes later he .... with a message from their mother. "Mum says if you .... now you can have some breakfast," he said.

9 So Carol .... with him. It was daylight now, so she .... the light in her room.

10 Downstairs, her father, Dennis, said, "What are you doing, Carol?"

"I'm .... my things .... , Dad," she said.

11 "Well, that's a good news!" he said. "Well done!" Dennis .... his coat and hat, ... of the house, ... his car and drove to his office.

12 Carol .... to her room again, and tried to .... the suitcase .... the cupboard. But it was to heavy for her. "Mum!" she shouted, "can you .... and help me?"

13 Victoria .... to her daughter's room, and together they .... the suitcase .... the cupboard. "That's very nice, dear," said her mother. "But you must stop now, ... those old clothes and .... some decent ones. Don't forget you're .... with Sue this morning."

14 So Carol .... the rest of her things .... in the cupboard, ... her old clothes, and .... a nice skirt and blouse.

15 Then she .... to see her friend Sue. She .... the bus at the corner of her street, and .... in the centre of town.

16 She............. the cafe, and saw Sue sitting at a table. "Hello, Carol," said Sue. "What have you been doing this morning?"

"I've been .... all my clothes .... in the right place," said Carol. "I'll never let it get so messy again as long as I live."

17 Sue had finished her coffee, and the waiter came and .... her cup ....

18 Carol asked for two more cups, and he soon .... and .... two coffees .... the table.

19 Sue .... the lid .... the sugar bowl, and .... two spoonfuls of sugar .... her cup.

20 A bird .... and landed on the edge of the table. " .... !" said Sue to the little bird, and it flew away.

ON IN UNDER (prepositions of place - 1)

Look at the picture, and study the text.

They are all in the living room.
Sally the cat is on the table,
and Winston is under the table.
Ophelia is in her bowl, and the
baby is under the chair. There
is a picture on the wall.

① Now look at these pictures, and complete
the sentences with IN, ON or UNDER.

1   Fred is .... the car.
2   Dennis is .... the car.
3   Sally is .... the car.
4   The ruler is .... the book.
5   The pencil is .... the book.
6   The pen is .... the book.
7   The files are .... the desk.
8   Winston is .... the desk.
9   The typewriter is .... the
    desk.

② Look at these pictures, and complete these sentences with IN or ON.

The watch is .... that shelf.
The meat is .... the oven.
John's .... the bathroom.
He's putting the plates .... the table.

There's some ice .... the glass.
The files are .... the desk.
Put the flowers .... that vase.
Look at that picture .... the wall.

True or False?

③ Read these sentences, and look at the picture. Three are true and three are false. Tick (✓) the true ones, and rewrite the false ones to make them true.

............1 The shirts are in the suitcase.

............2 The socks are on the suitcase.

............3 The belt is under the suitcase.

............4 The coat is in the suitcase.

............5 The swimsuit is on the suitcase.

............6 The shoes are under the suitcase.

Carol's Bedroom Is a Mess!

④ Look at the picture, and complete the sentences with IN, ON or UNDER.

1   Her trousers are .... the floor.
2   Her suitcase is .... the sofa.
3   Her T-shirt is .... the bed.
4   Her shoes are .... the bed.
5   Her swimsuit is .... the corner.
6   Her socks are .... the table.
7   Her new coat is .... the table.
8   Her books are .... the suitcase.
9   Her guitar is .... the sofa.
10 Her skirt is .... the drawer.
11 Her watch is .... the dressing table.
12 Her earrings are .... the bed.
13 Her handbag is .... the drawer.
14 Her towel is .... the bed.
15 And her gloves are .... the suitcase!

BEHIND   IN FRONT OF   BETWEEN   ABOVE   UNDER

(prepositions of place - 2)

Look at the picture, and study the text.

The table is between the armchair and the sofa, and the picture is on the wall above the piano.

Winston is in front of Uncle Victor, the cat is under the table, and Fred is behind the sofa!

BEHIND

IN FRONT OF

BETWEEN

UNDER

ABOVE

① Now look at this picture and complete these.

1   The carpet is .... the beds.
2   There's a suitcase .... the dressing table.
3   Victoria's shoes are .... the bed on the left.
4   The lamp is .... the dressing table.
5   Dennis is standing .... the wardrobe.

True or False?

② Read these sentences and look at the picture. Four are true and four are false. Tick (✓) the true ones, and rewrite the false ones.

.............1   The boy is between the trees.
.............2   The cat is under the car.
.............3   The book is under the chair.
.............4   The car is in front of the house.
.............5   The woman is in the car.
.............6   The bicycle is behind the house.
.............7   The kitchen is above the bathroom.
.............8   The chair is under the tree.

A Crash and a Traffic Jam

③ Read the paragraph, and fill the blanks with words from the box. Sometimes there will be more than one possibility.

above	under
in front of	between
behind	

I was driving down the road one day with my sister. The sun was .... us in the sky, and it was a lovely day. I started to overtake the bus .... me, when I saw a Volkswagen lying on its side. Three men were trying to lift the Volkswagen, because .... it there was the body of a man!

An ambulance was parked .... the Volkswagen, and .... it there was a police car. Some cars had stopped, and there was a policeman .... them holding up his hand to stop them.

There was a bridge .... the road, and standing on it were several people watching the scene. There was a lorry parked .... the bridge, and the driver was walking back to the scene of the crash.

I saw a blanket lying on the road; there was the body of another person .... it. There was an ambulance man standing .... the Volkswagen and the body lying on the ground.

Now the men were getting the body out from .... the car. They lifted the man up and put a stretcher .... him. Two men picked up the stretcher, one .... him and one .... Suddenly the man moved his arm; he was alive! .... them they had saved him.

I looked round and saw a long queue of cars .... us. .... us, the road was empty.

Keeping the Girlfriend Waiting

④ Read the paragraph, and fill the blanks with words from the box. Sometimes there will be more than one possibility.

above	under
in front of	between
behind	

The cinema in our town is in the main street, ... a hamburger place and an ice-cream parlour. On the first floor .... the ice-cream parlour, my accountant has her offices.

I drove up and saw my girlfriend standing .... the cinema waiting for me. So I drove into the carpark .... the cinema, left the car, walked to the front, and said: "Hi, Mavis!" "You're late!" she said.

"I'm sorry, I couldn't move my car because there was a cat .... it and he wouldn't come out. I was parked .... a Rolls Royce and a Jaguar, but the cat preferred to sleep .... my car!"

It's a Mad, Mad World: Jane Bond (008) in Action!

⑤ Look at the picture, and complete these sentences.

1 There's a snake .... her head.
2 There's a huge poisonous spider .... the bed.
3 .... the beds there is a hungry tiger.
4 There's a man with a gun .... the door.

AT TO FROM (prepositions of place and movement)

Look at the picture, and study the text.

It is Sunday today.
Fred is standing at the door,
Carol is walking to the bus stop,
and Uncle Victor is coming home
from the newsagent.

① Now complete these sentences with AT, TO or FROM.

From Monday to Friday...

1   Robert goes .... work at eight in the morning.
2   He comes home .... work about 6 o'clock.
3   Carol is usually .... home in the mornings.
4   She goes .... the clinic after lunch.
5   In the evening, she comes home .... the clinic about 8 pm.

USE
We say: She is at the office, etc.
She goes to the office, etc.
She is coming from the office, etc.
But **"home"** is different.
We say: He is **at home**.   OR   He is at **my** home.
She goes **home**. (to home)   OR   She's going to **my** home.
He phoned **from home**.   OR   He phoned from **my** home.

Good English?

② Read these six sentences. Three of them use AT, TO or FROM incorrectly. Tick (✓) the correct ones, and rewrite the wrong ones.

.... 1   Goodbye. I'm going to home.
.... 2   She drove from London to Manchester in two hours.
.... 3   I'll see you at home tonight.
.... 4   I'm meeting Robert to the corner of Oxford Street.
.... 5   Let's go at home!
.... 6   I'm taking him to my home.

More Practice

③ Complete these sentences with AT, TO, FROM or *nothing* (be careful with **home**!).

1 It takes half an hour to walk .... the house .... my office.
2 "I'm .... home this evening; can you come .... my house?"
3 The bus .... here .... the station takes about 15 minutes.
4 The bus going .... the station stops .... the bus stop, over there.
5 Robert is arriving soon; he's coming .... Sweden. He's staying ....
   Uncle Victor's house. He'll stay there two weeks. Then he's going .... Scotland
   to see a friend.

④ Complete these four dialogues as in the previous exercise.

1 "Where is Jane?"
   "She's .... the cinema; she's just phoned me .... there.
   She'll arrive .... home in a few minutes. She's walking .... home .... the
   cinema."
   "Will she be .... home this evening?"
   "Yes, Mary is coming round .... the house for the evening."

2 "Can you tell me the way .... the post office?"
   "Yes, walk .... the corner, and .... there you can see the post office. It's ....
   the end of the street."

3 "Excuse me, I want to go .... the Peabody Museum."
   "............. here you can take a bus .... the High Street. Get off the bus .... the corner
   of Smith Street. You can walk .... the museum .... there; it's .... the end of
   Smith Street."

4 "I'm tired. Let's go home."
   "I want to go to the pharmacy first. And .... there I want to go............. the new
    bookshop that just opened."
   "OK, I'll wait for you .... the corner."

It's a Mad, Mad World!

⑤ Look at the picture, and correct the three sentences which are false.

1 The lion is waiting for the lamb at
   the river.
2 The crocodile is swimming from the
   bank to the island.
3 The man is taking some bananas to
   the elephant.
4 The monkey is sitting at a table eating
   his supper.
5 The fish is flying from tree to tree.

MIXED EXERCISES   (units 35 – 37)

Here are six exercises which practise all the prepositions of place and movement in Units 35 – 37.

on   in   at   to   from   above   under
behind   in front of   between

① Complete these sentences with ON or IN (some alternatives are possible).

1   Is my book .... the bookshelf? No, it's .... the cupboard.
2   There's a notebook .... the desk, and you'll find a pencil .... the top drawer.
3   Robert was sitting .... a chair, and Carol was .... an armchair.
4   I waited .... the path; John was .... the house.
5   I got .... a bus, but Mrs Wellington got .... a taxi.
6   The little girl was lying .... bed, and her father sat .... the bed and told her a story.
7   We have four tennis balls; two are .... my hand, one is lying .... the court, and one is .... the long grass at the side of the court.

② Complete these sentences with ON, IN, AT or UNDER (some alternatives are possible).

1   Robert, put the plates .... the table.
2   Keep your wallet .... the pocket of your jacket.
3   In Paris, the "Metro" runs .... the centre of the city.
4   The picture is hanging .... the wall.
5   I'll wait for you .... the corner of the street.
6   He's standing .... the corner of the room.
7   The river Thames runs .... 15 bridges in London.
8   His bag's .... the bottom of the stairs; I'll take it up.
9   She is sitting .... the sofa.
10   I'll meet you .... the door of Westminster Abbey.
11   There's a waste paper basket .... my desk.
12   The "Chunnel" goes .... the English Channel from France to Britain.

③ Complete these sentences with IN, TO or AT and a word from the box (some alternatives are possible). Use A or THE if necessary.

theatre	station	office	school
airport	hospital	launderette	post office

1   "Where is Robert?"
     "He went .... to wash his clothes."
2   The play starts at 7.30; I can meet you .... at 7.15.
3   "Where's Fred?"
     "He's ...., I hope."
4   Let's have the meeting .... my .... at 10 o'clock.
5   "Rosie has had an accident on holiday; they've taken her .... in Madrid."
6   "My flight arrives at 8.45."
     "I can't meet you, but there are a lot of taxis ...."
7   The train doesn't leave for half an hour, so if you like we can walk ....
8   "I need some stamps."
     "You can buy them ...."

④ Complete these sentences with ABOVE, UNDER, BETWEEN, IN FRONT OF, BEHIND, FROM or TO (some alternatives are possible).

1   The roots of the tree go .... the house.
2   He got home .... the office about 7 o'clock at night.
3   "I finished the race in second place. .... me, in third place, was Veronica.
4   "Come and sit .... Sue and me."
5   .... the roofs of the houses you can see a forest of TV aerials.
6   You can't see the drains; they are .... the street.
7   It's about 2000 miles .... London .... New York.
8   "There's a lady with a big hat sitting .... me; I can't see!"
9   The Straits of Gibraltar run .... Spain and Morocco.
10 "There's a bird circling just .... your head."
11 "Look at that car .... us; there's a dog looking out of the back window."
12 The mezzanine is .... the ground floor and the first floor.

⑤ Complete these paragraphs with any of the prepositions listed at the top of the previous page.

1   .... Robert's room, there is a bed, a desk and a chair. The chair is............the desk and the bed. Robert keeps his shoes............. the bed. There is a ceiling light............. the desk, and ....the desk there is a notebook and a pen.

2   Hanging .... the wall .... the desk, there is a picture of five people in the tennis team. .... the front row are Brian and Peter. .... them, the back row, are the other three. Robert is............. the middle, ...his friends Gordon and Martin.

3   Robert goes .... a Tai Chi class on Wednesday evenings. He usually walks home .... the class, but sometimes he comes back .... the class .... Mike's car. Robert usually asks Mike to come in for a coffee, and Mike leaves his car .... the house.

4   Last Wednesday, Robert found Fred .... home sitting .... the TV. "Hey, Fred," he said, "can you go up .... my room and get my slippers? They're .... the bed."

5   Robert went ....the kitchen and made the coffee. He couldn't find the instant coffee, because it was .... the larder .... the top shelf .... a big tin of biscuits. He put a few biscuits .... a plate. At that moment there was a knock on the door.

6   There was a policeman outside. "Good evening, sir," he said. "Is that your car parked .... the house?" "The one .... the VW and the Citroen? It belongs to my friend Mike. He's .... the house."

⑥ Complete this paragraph with any of the prepositions listed at the top of the previous page.

.... the Johnsons' house there is a kitchen, a dining room and a living room .... the ground floor. .... the first floor there are three bedrooms and two bathrooms. One bathroom is .... the main bedroom, and the second bathroom is .... the other two bedrooms, ... the kitchen. The kitchen is .... the living room and the dining room. There is a driveway and a small garden .... the house, and a bigger garden .... the house. .... the big garden .... the back of the home, there is a big tree with a garden seat .... the grass .... it.

UP DOWN ACROSS ALONG (prepositions of movement –1)

Look at these pictures, and study the texts.

He is going
up the hill.

She is going
down the hill.

The ambulance
is going along
the road.

The train is
going across
the road.

① Now look at these pictures and complete these sentences with words from the box.

up	down
along	across

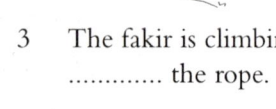

1 They are walking
.... the path.

2 The boy is going
.... the stream.

3 The fakir is climbing
.... the rope.

4 Pamela is going
.... the stairs.

5 They are walking
.... the river bank.

6 Edgar is walking
.... the road.

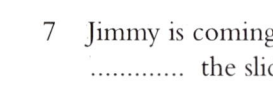

7 Jimmy is coming
.... the slide.

8 Brian is climbing
.... the ladder.

USE

Here are four prepositions of movement with pictures to illustrate their meaning.

 UP

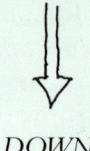 DOWN

ALONG

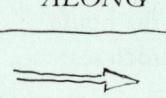

 *ACROSS*

Going In Different Directions

② Complete these sentences with UP, DOWN, ALONG or ACROSS. Sometimes there is more than one possibility.

1. There was so much traffic, we couldn't get .... the bridge.
2. The car drove .... the road for several miles.
3. Fred ran .... the road, and a car nearly hit him.
4. When Sally saw Winston, she ran .... the garden and climbed the tree.
5. "Robert, where are you?"
   "Upstairs."
   "Well come .... and eat your breakfast!"
6. The P & O ferries go .... the English Channel.
7. "The Grand Old Duke of York,
   He had ten thousand men,
   He marched them .... to the top of the hill,
   And he marched them .... again." (*Old English song*)

③ Look at the picture, and write a short reply to each question.

Example: Where is the cat going? *Up   the   tree*

1. Where is the girl going? ....
2. Where is the old lady walking? ....
3. Where is the boy running? ....
4. Where is the old man going? ....
5. Where is the car going? ....
6. Where is the dog running? ....
7. Where is the bus going? ....

It's a Mad, Mad World!

④ Are these pictures right? Rewrite the sentences, making them correct, as in the example below.

1. Look at that rabbit swimming across the river!

   Example: 1 *Rabbits don't swim across rivers; fish swim across rivers.*

2. Look at that penguin going up that tree!

   ....

3. Look at that fish going down a rabbit hole!

   ....

4. Look at that monkey walking across the ice!

   ....

ON   IN   OFF   OUT OF   (prepositions of movement –2)

Look at these pictures, and study the text.

Monday   Thursday

On Monday Carol put the flowers in the vase, and put the vase on the table; on Thursday she took the vase off the table, and took the flowers out of the vase.

IN   OUT OF   ON   OFF

① Complete these sentences with IN, ON, OFF or OUT OF.

1   "Put your passport .... the desk."
2   "Take your hands .... your pockets."
3   "Put your money .... your wallet."
4   "Take your feet .... the seat."

True or False?

② Here are two pictures and eight sentences. Four of the sentences are true and four are false. Tick (✓) the true ones, and rewrite the false ones.

..............1   She is taking the coat off the bed.
..............2   She is putting the pyjamas on the bed.
..............3   He is taking the towels out of the suitcase.
..............4   He is putting the shoes in the suitcase.

..............5   He is taking the printer off the desk.
..............6   She is putting the computer in the box.
..............7   He is taking the stapler out of the drawer.
..............8   She is putting the lunch in the box.

Which Direction?

③ Look at these pictures, and complete these sentences with IN, ON, OFF or OUT OF.

She's getting ....the car.

Take your things .... the table.

He's falling .... the river!

She's falling .... the window!

They're taking the pictures .... the wall.

They're putting them .... a box.

Take the potatoes .... the larder.

... and put them .... a pot.

Put your coat ....

Take your coat .... the hook.

④ Dennis, Victoria, Robert and Carol all came home at the same time. Whey did they do? Complete these sentence with IN, OUT OF, ON, or OFF.

1 Dennis took his hat .... and put it .... the table. Then he went .... bedroom and took his jacket and tie .... He took his dressing gown .... the wardrobe and put it ....

2 Carol took her coat .... Then she took a magazine .... her handbag, sat ....the armchair and started reading.

3 Robert had the house keys in his hand. He put them .... his pocket. He took his wallet .... his pocket, and put £5 .... the kitchen table.

4 Victoria went .... the kitchen. She had some shopping bags and she put them .... the table. She took the cheese and milk .... the bag and put them .... the refrigerator. Then she took the tea and coffee .... the bag and put them .... the cupboard. She put the bags .... the rubbish bin.

5 Then she put a pot of water .... the stove, and put a little oil and salt .... it. She took the spaghetti .... the cupboard, and put it .... the boiling water. She put the tomato sauce .... a small pot and put it .... the stove. She waited for ten minutes.

6 Then she took the spaghetti .... the pot, and put it .... four plates. She put the plates .... the table. She got the knives and forks .... the drawer, and then she walked .... the kitchen and called her family.

MIXED EXERCISES (units 39 – 40)

Here are four exercises which practise all the prepositions of movement in Units 39 – 40.

up   down   along   across   on   in   off   out of

① Complete these sentences with one of the prepositions in the box.

up   down
along   across

1   The helicopter went .... into the sky.
2   Walk .... this road to the corner, then turn left.
3   This oven is too hot; turn .... the gas.
4   "Don't run .... the road; you'll get hurt."
5   The boy put .... his hand and said, "I know the answer!"

6   They walked .... the hill to a small town at the bottom.
7   He looked .... the room and saw her on the other side.
8   We drove .... the highway for an hour and a half.
9   He climbed .... the tree to rescue the cat.
10 The ferry goes .... the river every hour.

11 Go .... this corridor, and you'll see the office on the right.
12 She closed the window and pulled .... the blind.
13 We walked .... a narrow path to the ruins below.
14 The lift went .... from the 10th to the 5th floor.
15 There's a bridge .... the river about five miles from here.

② Complete these sentences with one of the prepositions from the box.

on   in
off   out of

1   He took the meat .... the refrigerator, and put it .... the table.
2   "Come .... , and sit .... that chair."
3   He walked .... the house and got .... the car.
4   The cat climbed .... the window, and sat .... the carpet.
5   You can put your alarm clock .... the night table, and hang your trousers .... the wardrobe.
6   "Take your shoes .... the bed John; they're dirty!"
7   "I want to put this tablecloth .... the table. Carol, can you take that flowerpot .... ?"
8   He ran .... the house and got .... his bicycle.
9   "You can take your sweater .... It's warm in here; put it .... that chair."
10 "Please take the flowerpots .... the window shelf and put them .... the floor; I want to clean the windows."
11 "There are four napkins .... that drawer; can you take them .... the drawer and put them .... the table?"
12 "Where's Robert?"
    "He's taking the car .... the garage and putting it .... the road in front of the house.

③ Complete these sentences with any of the prepositions listed at the top of the previous page.

1   They went .... the building, and walked .... the stairs to the second floor.
2   "Can you take your books .... the table, please? I want to put the tablecloth ...."
3   She was driving .... the highway in her Mini-Minor, when she saw a dog walking .... the road!
4   "You can get .... the bus here, and get .... at the corner of Milsom Road."
5   They walked .... the hill to the top. They stayed there for a few minutes, and then they walked .... the hill to a small cafe in the village.
6   "Can you tell me the way to the castle?"
    "Yes, you walk .... this path for about a hundred yards, and you'll see a bridge. Go .... the bridge, and you'll see the castle."
7   "Take .... your coat and sit .... Would you like a cup of tea?"
8   She dressed, came .... her bedroom and walked .... the stairs to the kitchen.
9   The waiter brought the bill, so she took her wallet out of her handbag and put a £10 note .... the plate.
10 "Can you tell me where Accounts is?"
    "Yes, go .... this corridor to the last office. Just open the door and walk ...."
11 "Can you take the knives and forks .... the top drawer and put them .... the table?"
12 In the summer of 1992 they walked .... Andorra from one side to the other. It took three days. They went .... and .... plenty of hills, because Andorra is a very hilly country.
13 Maisie wanted to buy a white jumper to go with her navy blue skirt. She walked .... and .... Oxford Street all day, and went .... and .... about fifteen shops, but she just couldn't find a white long-sleeved jumper!
14 If you are a housewife in a big house, you spend the whole day going .... and .... the stairs, and .... and .... the rooms. You put plates .... the table before every meal, and you take them .... again afterwards. It never stops!

④ Complete this story with any of the prepositions listed at the top of the previous page.

Robert walked .... the main entrance, and went .... to the second floor. Then he walked .... the corridor to the Lawyer's office. He knocked .... the door and went ....

The young man quickly took his feet .... the desk and stood .... when Robert came .... "Good afternoon," he said, "please sit ...." Robert took his document wallet .... his briefcase and put it .... the young man's desk.

"You'll find my company's contract with Willis and Son .... the envelope. If you take it .... the envelope, you'll see the problem." Reluctantly, the young man reached .... the desk and picked .... the envelope. He took the contract .... the envelope, and looked at it. His face was white: .... the first page of the contract there was a different name!

He put the contract .... slowly and looked .... the desk at Robert. "You wrote this contract," said Robert, "and my boss put his signature .... it. He's very annoyed. Now you've got to go .... to the ground floor, walk .... the parking lot to the other building, go .... to the fourth floor, go .... the corridor to Willis's office, go .... and say you're sorry. OK?"

Without saying a word the young man got ...., walked .... the office, went .... the corridor and .... to the ground floor. He was .... his way to apologise!

AT   ON   IN   (prepositions of time -1)

Look at these three pictures, and study the texts below them.

A   *The baby was born*
at 2.15 am
on Monday 5th July,
in 1992.

B   *"On Christmas day*
in the morning!"

C   *They met*
on 20th June
at 4 o'clock
in the afternoon.

① Complete these sentences with AT, ON or IN.

1   "I'll see you .... lunch-time."
2   She came to see me .... 25th May.
3   We are going to Spain .... the summer.
4   They are arriving .... 4.15.
5   I was born .... 1972.
6   .... Saturdays I work .... the morning and play tennis .... the afternoon.

USE		
At	**On**	**In**
a time	*a day or date*	*a period of time*
at 6.45	on Monday	in the morning
at the right time	on 1st June	in January
	on the first day	in the spring
		in 1989

Note: We write: ... on 1st June
        We say: "... on the first of June"

Here are some more examples. Notice the use of "the" in the sentences on the right.

He's coming in March.   *He's coming in the spring.*
                                   He's coming in the afternoon

She's leaving on Wednesday.   *She's leaving on the last day.*
She's leaving at six.   *She's leaving at the right time.*

Good English?

② Here are eight sentences. Four of them have the wrong prepositions. Tick (✓) the correct ones, and
rewrite the wrong ones.

.... 1   I will see you <u>in</u> Wednesday.
.... 2   They came <u>on</u> 4th April.
.... 3   I go to the office <u>at</u> the morning.
.... 4   I like the weather <u>in</u> the summer.
.... 5   They are leaving <u>at</u> 8.30.
.... 6   Can I speak to you <u>on</u> dinner time?
.... 7   <u>On</u> 1992 we celebrated the 500-year anniversary of Columbus's voyage.
.... 8   "Come and see me <u>in</u> the evening."

Using the Article

③ Now complete these sentences with IN, ON or AT (+ THE if necessary).

1　I'll see you at home .... evening.
2　The film starts .... 8.45 pm.
3　We left .... wrong time, and we were late.
4　We're going to Corfu .... summer.
5　I can answer the letters .... afternoon.
6　I'm very busy; you've come .... wrong time.
7　" .... first day, we'll explain the programme for the week."
8　The next ferry leaves .... 11 am .... morning.

When?

④ Complete these sentences with ON, IN or AT (+ THE if necessary).

1　They started their journey .... 7.30.
2　She always gets up early .... morning.
3　I went to Paris .... spring.
4　We are going to the self-access centre .... Thursday.
5　The leaves turn brown .... autumn.
6　The course began .... March 3rd.
7　I went to Germany .... summer holidays.
8　We can have a party .... last day of the course.
9　She arrived .... wrong time, and waited for an hour.

⑤ Look at the information, and answer these questions with short answers, using IN, ON or AT (+ THE if necessary).

A

Psychotherapy:　Fridays (mornings)
(this week only:　Wednesday 2.30 pm)

1　What day do you usually go to psychotherapy? ....
2　What time of day do you go? ....
3　Are you going on the same day this week? ....
4　What time of day are you going? ....
5　What time is your appointment? ....

B

Winter break:　Bruges (February)
Summer break:　Acapulco (15th - 30th July)

1　What time of year are you going to Bruges? ....
2　Which month are you going in? ....
3　What time of year are you going to Acapulco? ....
4　Which month are you going in? ....
5　What date are you flying out? ....
6　What date are you flying back? ....

FOR FROM TO BEFORE AFTER (prepositions of time –2)

Look at these pictures, and study the text.

WORLD RECORD!

This afternoon Barney Bloggs stood on his head from noon to 8.15 pm. He remained in this position for a total of eight hours, fourteen minutes and thirty-six seconds. Before his great effort, Barney had a light meal. After it was over, he said, "The world is all upside-down!"

① Now complete this with FOR, FROM, TO, BEFORE or AFTER.

.... the great race, Sidney McDonald rested in his room. The marathon lasted .... three and a half hours, ... 2 pm .... 5.35 pm. .... it was all over, Sidney said, "Can I have a beer?"

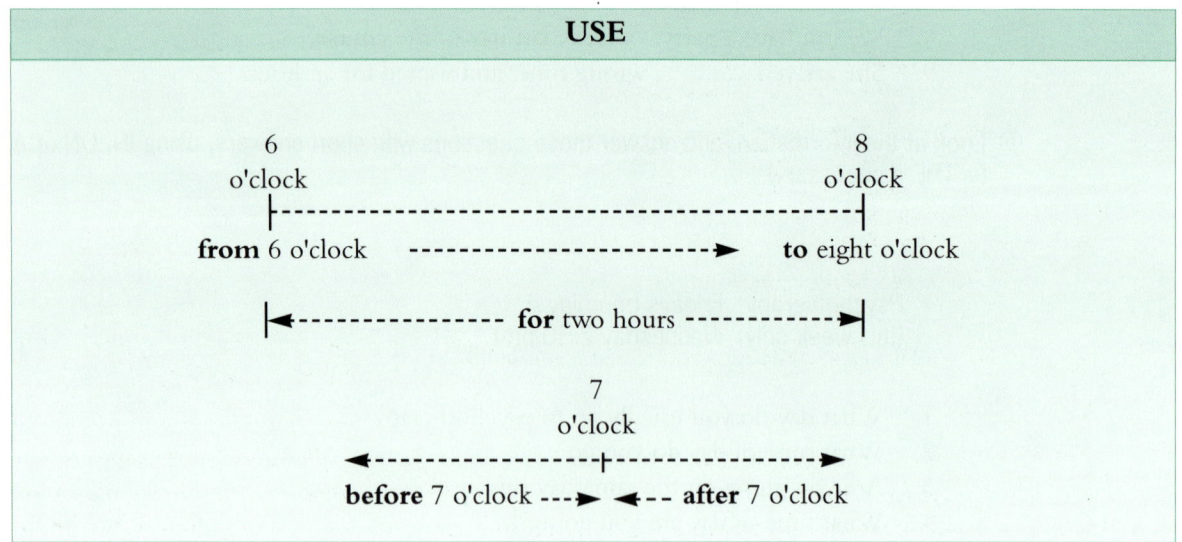

USE

6
o'clock

8
o'clock

from 6 o'clock ------------------------> **to** eight o'clock

|←---------------- **for** two hours ------------→|

7
o'clock

←----------------+----------------→
before 7 o'clock ---► ◄--- **after** 7 o'clock

Good English

② Look at the <u>underlined</u> parts of these sentences. Three of them are correct and three are wrong. Tick (✓) the correct ones, and rewrite the wrong ones.

.... 1 He cleaned his teeth <u>after</u> going to bed.
.... 2 Always check the petrol <u>before</u> you start the car.
.... 3 We stayed there for an hour, <u>to</u> four <u>from</u> five.
.... 4 They have coffee <u>from</u> 11 <u>to</u> 12 every day; it's the longest coffee break in the company!
.... 5 Susan and John got married three weeks <u>before</u> they met.
.... 6 After breakfast, we sat and talked <u>for</u> an hour.

The Young Life Of Olivia Bates

```
Born 1972, Brighton
Lived there 1972-1982
1982 Family moved to London
Secondary school 1983 - 1990
Lived in Paris 1991 (1 year, Jan - Dec)
Took a course, Sept 1991 - June1992
```

③ Complete these sentences with words from the box.

```
for        from        to
before     after
```

1   Olivia Bates lived in Brighton .... ten years, ... 1972 .... 1982.
2   A year .... the family moved to London, Olivia started secondary school. She went there .... seven years.
3   .... secondary school, she went to Paris .... a year .... January .... December.
4   .... she left Paris, she started a correspondence course. The course was .... Sept 1991 .... June 1992.
5   .... she finished the course, she moved back .... England. She lived with her father .... 1992 .... 1994.
6   .... she finished the course, she got a job.

George's Great Football Career

```
Born 1975, Bristol
Family moved to York 1978
Junior school 1980-1986
Football training 1984-1988
High school 1986 - now
Joined school team 1987
Broke his leg 1989
Left school team!
```

④ Complete these sentences with words from the box.

```
for        from        to
before     after
```

1   George lived in Bristol .... 1975 .... 1978, ... three years.
2   He started school .... the family moved to York.
3   He did football training .... two years, ... he left Junior school.
4   One year .... he started at high school he joined the school football team.
5   He played for the team .... 1987 .... 1989. Two great years!
6   His "career" ended in 1989 .... he broke his leg in a motorbike accident.

It's a Mad, Mad World!

⑤ These sentences are all false. Read and correct them if you can.

1   People sleep for twelve hours a day and cats for eight.
2   Christmas comes after the New Year.
3   A week has five days, from Monday to Friday.
4   In London in December, the day lasts for about 14 hours, from 6 am to 8 pm.
5   Secondary school comes before primary school.

MIXED EXERCISES (units 42 – 43)

Janet and Sam

Janet and Sam are very different people. She is organised; he is a mess.

① Complete these sentences about Janet and Sam, using the prepositions in the box.

in	on	at
from	to	for
before	after	

A   JANET

1   Janet wakes up .... 6.15 .... weekdays, but she stays in bed .... another fifteen minutes and gets up .... 6.30.
2   She has breakfast .... 7, but .... she has breakfast, she has a shower and gets dressed.
3   .... breakfast she watches the TV news .... fifteen minutes, ... 7.15 .... 7.30.
4   Then .... exactly 7.30, she puts on her coat and leaves the house. It takes ten minutes to walk to West Hampstead station, ... 7.35 .... 7.45.
5   She waits on the platform .... a few minutes, and catches the train .... Denmark Hill .... 7.50.
6.   .... 8.35 she arrives at Denmark Hill, and takes fifteen minutes to walk to the hospital .... 8.35 .... 8.50.
7   .... she starts work, she takes off her coat, and .... exactly nine o'clock she switches on the computer and works steadily until lunch-time.
8   .... 12.30 today her boss called her to his office, and .... 12.35 she got a pay rise.

B   SAM

1   Sam gets up .... a different time every day. He jumps out of bed, saying "Oh dear, I'm late", and he looks for clean clothes .... 10 minutes, but he can't find any.
2   He has breakfast .... fifteen minutes, then .... breakfast he remembers to have a shower, so he takes clothes off again.
3   .... the shower he puts his clothes on and switches on the television. There is a children's programme .... 8 .... 8.30, and he likes it. .... the programme he remembers to shave, so .... ten minutes he is in the bathroom again.
4   .... Monday he left the house .... 8.45, but .... he left he felt cold, so he went back for a coat .... 8.55. Then he ran to the station.
5   There was a train at 9.03, but he arrived .... 9.05, ... the train had left. So he waited .... 20 minutes for the next train.
6   He got to the office .... 9.55, and worked .... about an hour. .... that he felt tired, and .... 11.00 he went .... the cafeteria, and stayed there .... half an hour, ... 11.00 .... 11.30, talking to his friend Katherine.
7   .... 11.30, the boss called him to his office, and .... 11.35 he was fired!
8   .... he was fired, Sam went .... a cafe and sat there .... a couple of hour .... 11.45 .... about two o'clock.
9   .... 12.45 Janet went out for lunch. She saw Sam and sat with him .... an hour. .... she left, she gave him the address of another job.

The Olympic Games

② Complete these sentences about the Olympic Games, using prepositions from the box.

in	on	at
from	to	for
before	after	

A   HISTORY

1   The first Olympic champion was Coroebus, a sprinter, ... 776 BC.
2   They were held .... over a thousand years, ... 776 BC .... AD 393.
3   .... the first three hundred years, ... 776 BC .... 472 BC, all the competitions were held .... one day.
4   .... 472 BC they were held .... four days. .... the fifth day they presented the prizes and had a banquet.
5   .... 393, they were abolished by the Emperor Theodusius, ... Greece had lost its independence.
6   Baron Pierre de Coubertin was born .... New Year's Day, ... the year 1863.
7   .... 1892 he proposed the revival of the Olympic Games, but he had to wait .... two years, ... 1892 .... 1894, to get a response.
8   .... June 1894 the representatives of nine countries agreed to start the games in Paris .... 1900.
9   But Coubertin wanted to start the games .... 1900, and he moved them to Athens .... April 1896.
10   Coubertin was the President of the IOC .... 1896 .... 1925, ... 30 years.
11   The modern Olympics run .... 15 days, and the Winter Olympics .... 10 days.
12   .... the games, the organisers work 12 hours a day, then .... two weeks they don't sleep at all, and .... the games are finished they take a holiday!

B   BARCELONA 1992

1   The main Olympic Games are always held .... the summer, and in Barcelona they were held .... 18th July .... 3rd August.
2   The Winter Olympics were held in Abbeville, in January, ... 14th .... 20th.
3   The opening ceremony was held .... 18th July .... the afternoon, and lasted .... three hours, ... 2 pm .... 5 pm.
4   There were sporting events .... the morning and .... the afternoon every day. The finals of the 100 metres were held .... Sunday the 2nd, ... 3 pm.
5   .... the games there is intense preparation in the city .... about two years; .... the games, they do their arithmetic to see how much it cost!
6   The next games will be held .... 1996, in Atlanta, Georgia, in the USA.
7   .... the Atlanta games, ... 1994, the World Football Cup will be held.
8   The Olympic athletes are already in training, ... morning .... night.
9   Most athletics get up .... 6 or 6.30, train .... the morning, have a light lunch .... 1 o'clock, then watch training films .... the afternoon.
10   .... the month .... the games, most athletes train .... 10 hours a day.
11   .... the games they have a well – earned rest!

WITH BY FOR OF

Look at the picture, and study the texts.

See that girl with red hair?
And the house with big windows?
She broke that window with a stone.

That's typical of her!
Look, she's got a handful of stones!
Her poor mother will die of shame!

① Now complete these sentences with WITH or OF

1 He wrote his signature .... his left hand.
2 She took a bag .... toys home to the children.
3 Many people die .... hunger every year.
4 There's a man .... black hair over there.

Now study these texts.

They were going home
by bus, but they were
surrounded by hooligans,
so they contacted the
police by telephone.

"Yes, I'm phoning for information
about your office chairs."
"Yes, madam, what are the chairs for?"
"They're for the reception area."
"Yes, madam, we can sell you two for £85."

USE

Here are some of the ways we use these prepositions:

with red hair	*with* big windows	*with* his left hand	*with* me
blue eyes	pictures	a hammer	Robert
typical *of*	handful *of*	*by* fax	*for* information
kind	pile	phone	you
die	bag	bus	£100
glass		train	his school

② Now complete these sentences with BY or FOR.

1 We usually go to school .... train, but today we walked.
2 He sold his old computer .... £100.
3 Send them a message .... fax, if you want an answer today.
4 These new cushions are .... the sofa.

Good English?

③ Look at the underlined prepositions. Four of them are correct and four are wrong. Tick (✔) the correct ones, and rewrite the wrong ones.

.... 1 You can cut the bread <u>by</u> a knife.

.... 2 Do you like tea <u>of</u> milk? Here is a jug <u>of</u> milk.

.... 3 This play is <u>by</u> Shakespeare.

.... 4 I bought a coke <u>by</u> you to have <u>with</u> your sandwich.

.... 5 I bought these shoes <u>by</u> £20.

.... 6 I've got a pound <u>of</u> apples.

Mixed Bag

④ Complete the sentences with appropriate prepositions from the box.

by	with
for	of

1 He caught the ball .... his left hand.
2 "This is a picture .... my mother."
3 I usually go to work .... bus.
4 We must get some medicine .... her cold.
5 How kind .... you to help me!
6 Can you walk .... me to the corner?
7 This coat was designed .... Diorelli.
8 .... more information, write to this address.
9 There's a child .... a dirty face sitting in the corner.
10 I don't like the colour .... her dress.
11 We got married on the 27th .... January.
12 She went to Miami .... plane.
13 I travelled .... him to Paris.
14 Send the message .... fax; it's quicker.
15 If I don't have a drink soon, I shall die .... thirst!
16 I'm looking for a book .... a green cover.
17 What will you buy .... the money?
18 Look, I've got a present .... you!
19 She went .... Robert in his car.
20 He plays football .... the university.

True or False?

⑤ Look at these pictures, and study the texts. If a text is not true, change it.

1 He is going with his mother by plane.

2 This hoover is for cleaning the windows.

3 He is reading a book by Shakespeare for his exams.

AT HOME (prepositions and nouns)

Look at these pictures, and study the texts.

Peter is on business.
The young couple are on holiday.
The receptionist is on duty.

Mum's at her office,
Dad's at home, and
the kids are at school.

① Now match the two halves of these sentences.

1	There is a policeman in uniform at the corner;	A	the company pays your fare.
2	When you travel on business, ...	B	and I like to stay at home.
3	He's 20 years old, and he's carrying a pile of books;	C	he spends half his day at the hospital.
4	My father is a doctor;	D	to a beach or to the mountains?
5	Where do you like to go on holiday, ...	E	he's on duty.
6	I come home tired in the evenings, ...	F	he must be at the university.

Now study these texts.

Carol is in a mess; she didn't go by train.
Fred is in trouble; he didn't learn the poem by heart.
Robert is in danger; he left the car door open by mistake.

② Now match the two halves of these sentences.

1	If you want to travel cheaply, ...	A	and spilt water on the floor.
2	You'll be in trouble with the teacher	B	I can't make sense of them!
3	He dropped the glass by mistake, ...	C	by heart, I'm afraid.
4	The climber was in danger	D	you'd better go by bus.
5	You'll have to learn the verbs	E	when he dropped his rope.
6	These papers are in a mess;	F	if you don't study!

Good English?

③ Look at the underlined prepositions. Four of them are correct and four are wrong.
Tick (✓) the correct ones, and rewrite the wrong ones.

.... 1 You can get there easily <u>by</u> bus.
.... 2 I think Robert is <u>in</u> home.
.... 3 If you are <u>in</u> difficulties, you can ask for help.
.... 4 Some students learn whole passages <u>on</u> heart.
.... 5 He broke the vase <u>by</u> accident.
.... 6 Your desk is <u>into</u> a mess!
.... 7 When we were <u>in</u> holiday we had a wonderful time.
.... 8 If you ask the man <u>on</u> duty at the desk, he'll help you.

④ Complete these sentences with a word from the box, and ON, AT, IN or BY

duty	business	heart
a factory	underground	trouble

1   Actors have to learn long plays ....
2   Uncle Victor was always .... at work; his boss didn't like him.
3   Robert flew to Tokyo .... ; he had to meet the sales people from Panasonic.
4   In London the traffic is very heavy, so it's usually quicker to travel ....
5   Today Victoria is spending the day .... , because she is teaching her pupils about working life.
6   The policeman is .... until 6 pm.

danger	mistake	school
holiday	college	a mess

7   Fred is not a tidy boy; his room is usually .... !
8   One day, Carol put on two different coloured socks .... ; have you ever done that?
9   Fred is thirteen; he'll stay .... for another five years.
10   Victoria likes to go .... once a year to a sunny beach.
11   Firemen take great risks, and they are often ....
12   Carol is 20 years old and she is still .... ; she has two more years to do.

It's a Mad, Mad World!

⑤ Look at these 12 figures, and complete the sentences with ON, AT, IN or BY and a suitable word or phrase.

Number 1 is ....

Number 2 is ....

Number 3 is ....

Number 4 is ....

Number 5 is ....

Number 6 is ....

Number 7 is ....

Number 8 is cutting his finger ....

Number 9 is ....

Number 10 is ....

Number 11 is travelling ....

Number 12 is learning a poem ....

READY FOR (adjectives and prepositions)

Look at these pictures, and study the texts.

She's <u>good at</u> painting.
She's <u>bad at</u> singing.
She's <u>terrible at</u> Maths.

Are you <u>ready for</u> supper?
Fruit is <u>good for</u> you.
Smoking is <u>bad for</u> everybody

① Complete these sentences with expressions from the ones <u>underlined</u> above.

　　1　A lot of sweets are .... children's teeth.
　　2　He's not very .... Biology (40/100), and he's .... Chemistry; he got zero!
　　3　I'm not .... you yet, can you wait a few minutes?
　　4　He's .... his job, and his boss likes him.

Look at these pictures, and study the texts.

I'm <u>afraid of</u> the boss;
he's <u>suspicious of</u> everybody.
I'm <u>fond of</u> my colleagues,
but we're all <u>jealous of</u> Mary
because the boss likes her.

Susan is <u>generous to</u> her sister
and <u>friendly to</u> everybody.
But Michael is <u>rude to</u> everyone,
and he is <u>cruel to</u> his dog.

② Complete these sentences with suitable expressions from the ones <u>underlined</u> above.

　　1　Jane is .... her cat.　She is never .... to it or treats it badly.
　　2　If the parents have a favourite son, the other children will be .... him.
　　3　You mustn't be .... strangers; speak more politely!

Robert, Carol and Fred

③ Here are some things that Robert, Carol and Fred have said. Match what they say to the descriptions below.

				Descriptions
1	*Fred*	"Go away, Carol; I can't stand you!"	A	She's generous to Fred.
2	*Carol*	"Here, Fred, I've bought you a present."	B	He's good at chess.
3	*Robert*	"Why do you always give things to Carol and not to me?"	C	He's being rude to Fred.
4	*Carol*	"Why is that man always looking at me?"	D	She's suspicious of the man.
5	*Robert*	"I played Uncle Victor today, and I won."	E	He's jealous of Carol.

				Descriptions
6	*Carol*	"Robert, help, there's someone following me!"	A	He is terrible at spelling.
7	*Fred*	"I got 2 out of 10 today."	B	He is sometimes cruel to Sally.
8	*Carol*	"Fred, don't you touch those cigarettes!"	C	She thinks smoking is unhealthy for you.
9	*Robert*	"Well, I've packed all my bags."	D	He's ready for his holiday.
10	*Carol*	"Fred, leave that cat alone!!"	E	She's afraid of the man.

				Descriptions
11	*Fred*	"I love you, Sis!"	A	She's bad at bridge.
12	*Carol*	"I can't play this stupid game!"	B	He is friendly to people.
13	*Robert*	"I drink half a pint of this every day."	C	He is fond of his sister.
14	*Fred*	"Hello, everyone, are you OK?"	D	He thinks milk is good for you.

Mixed Bag

④ Now complete these sentences, using the appropriate expression from the boxes and AT, OF, FOR or TO.

ready	jealous
fond	cruel good

A 1 Parents are usually .... their children.
   2 You must never be .... animals.
   3 Pele was very .... football!
   4 "Are you .... your next patient, doctor?"
   5 He was .... all his wife's friends.

friendly	good	generous
afraid	terrible	

B Fred is a good lad. He has a nice smile, and he's always .... people. He's not very
.... Maths, and he's .... Spelling (2/10 in his last test!). But he's very brave, and he's
not .... anything. He likes giving things to friends; he's very .... them.

rude	suspicious
bad	

C 1 Don't let's drink too much coffee; it's .... you.
   2 I'm rather .... these good exam results; do you think he cheated?
   3 I only asked if I could borrow some money, and he was quite .... me!

MIXED EXERCISES (all prepositions)

In these exercises, you will use all these prepositions you have met so far.

Place:
in   on   under   behind
between   above   in front of

Movement:
in   on   off   out of   to   from   up
down   along   across

Time:
at   on   in   from   to
before   after

Other:
with   by   for   of

Prepositions and nouns: on duty   by mistake etc.
Adjectives and prepositions: good at   ready for etc.

Robert's New Post

① Robert recently got a new job in Conran's. He normally works .... nine .... five, but he usually finishes late .... Wednesdays, and sometimes he goes .... the office .... Saturday. He leaves the house .... 8.30, walks .... the bus stop, and catches a No. 13 bus .... Green Park. Then he walks .... Picadilly .... Hyde Park Corner. That's where his office is.

.... lunch-time he usually goes .... the cafeteria, which is .... the basement. He often has a sandwich .... lunch, and a glass .... sparkling water. .... lunch he sometimes goes .... and walks .... the park .... his friend Roger.

Carol and Sam Go To the Films

② Carol and her boyfriend Sam often go .... the films. Last Saturday night they went to see "Gold and Silver", ... Sean Connery .... the main part. The film started .... 6.15, so they got there twenty minutes .... that. They bought their tickets, and waited. First they watched the advertisements and the shorts, and .... that they saw the main film.

.... the film, they came .... the cinema, and walked .... the road to the corner. They turned right, and walked .... a short hill .... a little square which they like. They walked .... the square .... a little cafe .... the trees .... the other side. There, they sat .... and had a coffee. .... that, Sam walked .... Carol .... her house.

Dennis Goes For a Drive

③ .... Wednesday Dennis drove .... Hampton .... Winford .... business. He had breakfast .... home. Then he got .... his car and left .... 8 am. About halfway .... Hampton and Winford, he was driving slowly .... a big lorry when he saw a rabbit running .... the road. He slowed down because he was afraid .... hitting the rabbit, but the driver .... him was half asleep, and crashed into him. They stopped and Robert got .... the car and spoke .... the man.

Robert's Habits

④ Every morning, ... he goes to his office, Robert has a cup of coffee .... home. He works all morning .... nine .... one. He has lunch .... one, and .... lunch he usually goes to see one .... the shops. Conran's have a chain .... shops, and Robert visits them .... business.

Victoria Also Goes For a Drive

⑤ One afternoon .... school, Victoria was driving .... a city street .... 70 kilometres an hour, when she looked .... the mirror and saw a police car .... her. She was not very good .... driving, and the policeman asked her for her licence. "Oh dear, it's not .... my wallet," she said, and the policemen said, "You'll have to come .... us .... the station, madam." She wasn't afraid .... the police, because she had a licence; she had left the licence .... school .... mistake. The policeman was not very friendly .... her, and Victoria thought: "I'm .... trouble; I'm going to be late .... my meeting!"

Mixed Bag

⑥ 1 Smoking is bad .... you.
2 Some people are afraid .... dogs.
3 This book was written .... Wilbur Smith.
4 The sun was shining .... the sky .... their heads.
5 He had learnt the speech .... heart, so he put his notes .... the table and did not look at them.
6 He did not see the dog because it was asleep .... the floor .... the table.
7 He was suspicious .... a man standing .... the street, so he phoned the police .... 8.30 pm.
8 Genghis Khan was generous .... his friends and cruel .... his enemies.
9 "Take your coat .... and put it .... that chair, if you like."
10 Dennis is very fond .... Victoria, but when they were younger, he was sometimes jealous .... her.
11 .... spring the flowers come .... , but .... autumn the leaves turn brown and fall .... the trees.
12 .... 1991 I went .... holiday to Greece. I am bad .... driving, so I went .... plane. I stayed there .... three weeks, and came back .... Monday 12th August.
13 Take this medicine; it'll be good ...:......... you.
14 People who climb mountains must be ready .... anything, and they are often .... danger.
15 Travelling .... train is often quicker than going .... car; the slow way to go is .... foot.
16 You should be friendly .... strangers, and you mustn't be suspicious .... them or rude .... them.

Where Are They?

⑦ Look at this picture of the family, and complete the sentences.

1 Dennis is standing .... the back .... Victoria and Robert.
2 Fred is sitting .... Victoria, and Carol is sitting .... of Dennis. Winston is lying .... the floor .... Fred and Carol!

A(N) and THE (definite and indefinite)

Look at the picture, and study the text.

"Look! There's an elephant."
"It's not an elephant; it's a giraffe."
"The elephants are over there, near the monkey house."

"Dad, what does that man do?"
"He's a zoo attendant."

① Complete these with A, AN or THE.

1   Look, I have .... banana and .... apple. .... apple is OK, but .... banana is bad.
2   Paris is .... big city; France is .... beautiful country. Paris is .... capital of France.
3   .... sun is very strong; can you close .... curtain?
4   Robert is .... accountant; his mother is .... school teacher.

USE

We use **A/AN** on the first occasion:
   Look! There's an elephant! (The first time)
... and when we don't know exactly what we are referring to:
   I want an ice cream. (We don't know which one.)

We use **THE** on the second (or later) occasion:
   You can give the elephant a banana. (The second time)
... and when we know what we are referring to:
   Can you close the window? (We know which window.)

> A or AN?
> *Why A?*
> a book   a radio
> a sandwich   a coke
>
> *Why AN?*
> an idea   an elephant
> an apple   an orange

FORM

	"new"	"old"
Singular	a(n)	the
Plural		the

Good English?

② Look at the underlined parts of these sentences. Three of them are correct and three are wrong. Tick (✓) the correct sentences, and rewrite the wrong ones.

.... 1   Can I make a phone call, please?
.... 2   Yes, a telephone is over there.
.... 3   Susan Parkman is doctor.

.... 4   Yesterday I saw a woman in
....   an ambulance.
.... 5   He is eating a orange.

A(n) and The

③ Complete these with A(N) and a noun from the box.

> policeman   actor
> architect   pianist   singer

1   She plays a musical instrument; she is 4   He sometimes directs traffic; he is ....
2   She sings with a pop group; she is 5   She designs buildings; she is ....
3   He works in the theatre; he is ....

④ Complete these with THE and a noun from the box.

> airport   pharmacy
> post office   doctor

1   I had a stomach ache, so I went to see ....
2   He want some stamps, so he walked to ....
3   We were flying to Milan at 2, so we went to .... at 12.30.
4   She want to buy some aspirins, so she went to ....

Sammy

⑤ Complete these two passages with A or THE.

1   Sammy has .... radio. There is .... park near his house, with .... wooden bench near .... small lake. There are fish in the lake.

2   This morning Sammy got up, listened to .... radio for a few minutes. Then he walked to............ park and sat on .... bench. He could see .... fish, who were swimming in .... lake.

Geography

⑥ Complete these sentences with A(N), THE, and a word from the box.

> island   capital   city
> country   river

1   Glasgow is ....
2   .... of Canada is Ottawa.
3   Costa Rica is .... in Central America.
4   .... Seine flows through Paris.
5   Mozambique is .... in the Indian Ocean.

Mixed Bag

⑦ Complete these sentences with A(N), THE or nothing.

1   "You're not well; I'm going to call .... doctor!"
2   "Do you know .... woman sitting over there?"
     "Yes, she's .... woman I'm going to marry!"
3   Thee was .... accident yesterday, when .... car hit .... child.
4   I have two children, ... boy and .... girl. .... girl works in a bank and .... boy is a computer programmer.

⑧ There are twelve articles missing in these sentences. Can you put them in? The first is done for you.

There was *a* young man outside my office, waiting for me with file in his hand. He gave me file. He was wearing blue suit and red tie, but suit was torn and tie was dirty. He had briefcase and umbrella, but umbrella was very old and briefcase didn't have handle.

A   SOME   (indefinite: singular, plural and uncountable –2)

Look at these pictures, and study the texts.

The first woman wants to buy some winter clothing, and the second wants some jewellery.

*I'd like to see some woollen
skirts and a winter coat, please.*

*I want to buy a necklace
and some earrings.*

① Complete these sentences with A, AN or SOME.

1   Brian went to the clothing store and bought .... blue jeans, ... blue shirt,
.... socks, ... hat, and .... umbrella.
2   Sue went to the supermarket and bought .... oil, ... potatoes, ... new frying
pan, ... sausages, ... bread and .... pound of cheese.

USE

A   We use **A/AN** with nouns in the singular (see Unit 49 for definite and indefinite).
We do not use singular nouns alone:
    Would you like a drink?   (*Not*: ✗ Would you like drink?)

We use **A/AN** with professions:
    Mr Meeson is an architect.   (*Not*: ✗ Mr Meeson is architect.)
    Ms Jones is a company executive. (*Not*: ✗ Ms Jones is company executive.)

We use **A/AN** with descriptions:
    Brian Smith is a tall man.   (*Not*: ✗ Brian Smith is tall man.)
    Tokyo is a big city. (*Not*: ✗ Tokyo is big city.)

B   We use **SOME** with nouns in the plural, and with uncountable nouns:
    There are some eggs in the refrigerator.
    Can you buy some butter and some olive oil?

Good English?

② Look at the underlined parts of these sentences. Three of them are correct and three are wrong.
Tick (✓) the correct ones, and rewrite the wrong ones.

....   1   He was carrying a folder and a books.
            2   Can I have some milk in my tea?
....   3   I would like some postcard and a airmail stamps.
            4   I'd like a piece of cake.

Going On Holiday

③ Complete these sentences with A or SOME.

1   When you go on .... trip, what do you usually take with you?
2   Well, I usually take .... suit, ... shirts and .... socks.
      If it's winter I take .... warm clothing, such as .... coat and .... scarf, and
      .... thick pullovers.
3   Do you take .... hat?
      No, not usually. Well, I take .... sun hat to the beach, ... water to drink and
      .... towel. And I take .... swimming costume and .... suntan lotion.
4   If I'm going alone, I always take .... magazines and .... book. I always take
      .... pen, because on the second day I usually have .... free time to write postcards.
5   If I'm going with .... friend, then we usually go out in the evening to have .... cool
      drink or buy .... presents for the family. I usually have .... good time.

Going To the Shops

④ Sammy is going to the shops; Lisa is telling him what to get. ·
    Complete her instructions with the right items from the box for each shop, and A(N) or SOME.

fruit	toothbrush	stamps	aspirins
nails	airmail envelopes	big lettuce	hammer

1   I want you to go to the pharmacy, and buy me .... and ....
2   I want you to go to the fruit and vegetable market, and buy me .... and ....
3   I want you to go to the post office, and buy me .... and ....
4   I want you to go to the hardware store and buy me .... and ....

It's a Mad, Mad World!

⑤ Complete each sentence with A or SOME and a noun.

I want .... ; these are too tight for me.

I need .... ; these are broken.

I'm looking for .... ; I don't like this one.

I'm looking for .... ; this one is torn.

I want .... ; this one is too big for me.

I need .... ; these have got holes in them.

SOME and ANY

Look at the picture, and study the text.

"Have you got some/any lemonade?"
"Yes, and I've got some coke for the kids."
"Right. Now, we've got some sandwiches and some cake, but we haven't got any biscuits.
Have we got some/any tea?"
"No, and we haven't got any coffee."

① Complete these sentences with SOME or ANY.

1   I haven't got .... money.
2   Do you want to buy .... sandwiches?

3   There's .... cheese in the fridge.
4   I don't need .... airmail stamps.

USE

We use **SOME/ANY** with plural and uncountable nouns:
There was some tea and some biscuits on the table.
There wasn't any coffee and there weren't any cakes.

We use **SOME** or **ANY** with interrogatives:
Would you like some/any tea?

② Now complete this table according to the USE box above.

	Plural	**Uncountable**
Affirmative	.... books	.... bread
Negative	(not)............books	(not) .... bread
Interrogative	............./	............./
	.... books?	.... bread?

Good English?

③ SOME or ANY are underlined seven times in these sentences. Three of them are right, two of them are wrong, and two of them have another alternative. Tick (✔) the correct ones, rewrite the wrong ones, and put in the alternatives on the right.

Alternatives?

.... 1   He heard some rock music and any songs.   _____
.... 2   Did you put some milk in my tea?   _____
.... 3   He bought some shirts and some coat.   _____
.... 4   Do you want any bread?   _____
.... 5   He didn't want any tea.   _____

Dennis and Victoria Go Shopping

④ Complete these sentences with SOME or ANY (or both).

1 First they went to the vegetable department. They bought .... potatoes and .... cabbage, and .... carrots, but they didn't buy .... onions, ... courgettes or .... peas.

2 Then they went to the meat department. They bought .... lamb chops and .... sausages, but they didn't buy .... steak. Dennis wanted to buy .... lamb for Sunday lunch, but Victoria said: "Let's buy .... fish for Sunday."

3 They went to the fish department, where they bought .... nice cuts of salmon for Sunday, and .... cod fillets to make fish and chips. But they didn't buy .... shrimps or .... tuna fish.

4 Then they went to the dry goods department. "Do you want .... chocolate?" asked Dennis. "Yes," said Victoria, so Dennis bought .... chocolate and .... biscuits. They didn't get .... honey, because they had .... at home. "Is there .... jam in the fridge?" asked Victoria. "Yes, there is .... ," said Dennis.

5 Then they went to toiletries. Dennis bought .... toothpaste. He didn't buy .... razor blades, but he bought .... shaving cream and Victoria bought .... cotton wool and .... bars of soap. "Shall I buy .... face cream?" thought Victoria. "No, I won't buy .... here; I can buy .... in the Body Shop. It's cheaper."

6 Finally, they went to the bakery, where they bought .... baguettes, ... brown bread and .... little cakes for tea. They didn't get .... cheese. "Shall I get .... eggs?" asked Victoria. "No, we've got .... ," said Dennis.

Building a Tree House

⑤ Robert is helping Fred to build a tree house. Complete the sentences, using SOME or ANY and a word from the box.

| wood | paint |
| nails | brushes |

Robert   OK, to build a house we'll need ...., a hammer and .... That's all.

Fred   We'll also need ...., because I want to paint it green, and we'll need .... to do the painting with.

Robert   OK, but we won't need to buy .... green ...., because there's .... in the garage. I think it's green. And we won't have to buy ...., because there are two in the garage with the paint.

It's a Mad, Mad World! (With Apologies To Lewis Carroll)

⑥ Complete these sentences with SOME or ANY.

"Have .... wine," the March Hare said.
"I don't see .... wine," Alice remarked.
"There isn't .... ," said the March Hare.

"Oh," said Alice. "Then can I have .... tea?"
"Yes, if you want to," said the Mad Hatter.
"But there isn't .... in the pot," said Alice.
"In that case you can't have .... !"

A SOME ANY

Look at the picture, and study the texts.

"I'd like some writing paper please, two packets."
"Yes, madam, do you want any envelopes?"

*"Yes, I'll have some envelopes, but I don't need any
milk. Oh, and I want a newspaper and a copy
of the TV Times."*

① Now complete these sentences with A(N), SOME or ANY.

1   I'd like you to bring me .... ice cream and .... magazines.
2   I'd like to listen to .... music; how about going to .... concert?
3   "I need .... help." "I'm sorry, I haven't got .... spare time."
4   We need .... furniture for the dining room; .... table and .... chairs.

USE

We use **A** with singular nouns:
    Would you like *a* biscuit or *a* piece of cake?

We use **SOME** with plural and uncountable nouns **in the affirmative**:
    There was *some* tea and *some* biscuits on the table.

We use **ANY** with plural or uncountable nouns **in the negative**:
    There wasn't *any* tea and there weren't *any* biscuits.

We use **SOME** or **ANY** in the interrogative:
    Would you like *some/any* tea?

FORM

SINGULAR, PLURAL and UNCOUNTABLE
    This is *SINGULAR*:   a book   a man
    This is *PLURAL*:   three books   some men

    This is *not singular*, and *not plural*: air   some water
                                               some meat   music
    You cannot count these items; they are UNCOUNTABLE nouns.

---

② Now complete this table.

	Singular	Plural	Uncountable
Affirmative	..... book	..... books	.....bread
Negative	..... book	(not) ... books	(not)... bread
Interrogative	..... book?	...../	...../
		.....books?	.....bread?

Good English?

③ Look at the underlined parts in these sentences. Two of them are right, two are wrong, and one has another alternative. Tick (✔) the correct ones, rewrite the wrong ones, and put in the alternative on the right.

Alternatives?

..............1 I went to a concert and heard <u>beautiful music</u>. _____

..............2 Have you ever heard <u>a really good violinist</u>? _____

..............3 There will be <u>some beautiful concerts</u> this winter. _____

..............4 I am reading <u>some book</u> in French for school. _____

..............5 Do you have <u>some time</u> to help me with this? _____

The Empty Shop

④ This corner shop is always empty! Rajiv is not a good shopkeeper, and he forgets to order. Complete the sentences with A, SOME or ANY.

1 Good morning, Rajiv. I'd like .... milk, ... can of diet coke, ... copy of *The Times* and .... stamps.

2 Sorry, sir, I haven't got .... milk, and I haven't got .... coke, but I have ....stamps. Do you want first class or second class?

3 I'd like .... second class stamps, please, about £5.

4 Sorry, sir, I haven't got .... second-class stamps, only first-class stamps.

5 Oh. Can I have .... copy of The Times, please?

6 Sorry, sir, I haven't got .... newspapers today.

7 Oh. Have you got .... postcards?

8 Yes, sir, I've got .... nice postcards, over there.

Making a Film

Peter Hall and Brian Wills are going to make a film about Mother Teresa. It'll be cheap, because they haven't got much money!

⑤ Complete each sentence with a word from the box, and A, SOME or ANY. (*Tip:* Read all the sentences before doing the exercise.)

| time actors star |
| camera director |

1 OK, first we'll need .... to direct the film.

2 Then we'll need .... We must have a famous actress for the part of Mother Teresa.

3 Then we'll need .... to play the other parts.

4 Right. And we'll need .... and a cameraman, to shoot the film.

5 This will take .... - about six weeks, I think.

| extras script writer lighting equipment |
| sound equipment location |

6 Shall we need .... ? No, I don't think so; we can use natural light.

7 Who will write the story? We'll need ....

8 We shall have to decide on .... somewhere in India.

9 But we'll need .... to record the sound.

10 We won't need .... ; we can use the people from the villages.

ONE TO A HUNDRED (numbers)

Look at these pictures, and study the texts.

"What is your phone number?"
"Nine four three,
seven oh six one."

"When did George Orwell die?"
"On the twenty-first of January, nineteen fifty."

① Write out these telephone numbers.

645 4297 ....   231 3722 ....

303 6642 ....(double six...)...........   808 7516 ....

② Write out sentences like this.

Example: They were in Montreal in ~~nineteen seventy-six.~~ ....
   1   They were in Barcelona in ....
   2   They were in Seoul in ....
   3   They were in Moscow in ....
   4   They were in Los Angeles in ....
(Question: What were "they"?)

③ Look at the example, then complete the sentences.

Example: ~~When is mid-summer day?~~
........~~the twenty-fourth of June~~........

   1   When is New Year's Day?
....

   2   When is New Year's Eve?
....

   3   When is Christmas day?

....

Some ordinal numbers

first	eleventh
second	twelfth
third	
fourth	twentieth
fifth	twenty-fifth
sixth	
	thirtieth
	thirty-first

USE

We say TELEPHONE NUMBERS as individual numbers:
   four three one, one five nine oh.
We say YEARS in pairs:
   nineteen ninety-four
We say DATES with ordinal numbers (first, second, etc.):
   The first of March   The twenty-fifth of June
We write:
   1st March   25th June

Spelling

④ Complete this table with the numbers 1 - 20. Two have been done for you.

3 letters	4 letters	5 letters	6 letters	7 letters
....	....	*seven*	....	....
....	....	....	....	....
....	....	....	....	....
....			8 letters	9 letters
			thirteen	....
			....	
			....	
			....	

Numbers and Ordinal Numbers

⑤ Complete the following sentences.

She asked him to marry her five times.
The .... time, he said: "Definitely not."
The .... time, he said: "No."
The .... time, he said: "Perhaps."
The .... time, he said: "I'll think about it."
The .... time, he said: "Yes."

⑥ These people all live in a block of flats in London. Their telephone numbers are secret. Which are they?
(*Clue*: Look at the first two numbers of each telephone.)

The Occupants
Boris Yeltsin (born 1931)
Margaret Thatcher (born 1925)
François Mitterand (born 1916)
Ringo Starr (born 1940)

The Telephone Numbers
407 6915   256 7803
163 3184   316 1403

⑦ Look at these addresses, and say where the places are.

Example: "5th and 42nd" ...*fifth Avenue and forty-Second Street.*..........
"1st and 25th"   ....
"10th and 23rd"   ....
"2nd and 31st"   ....
"3rd and 33rd"   ....
"7th and 30th"   ....
"4th and 28th"   ....
"9th and 21st"   ....

It's a Mad, Mad World: Mad Maths!

⑧ These are nearly all wrong. Can you correct them?

Adding: 1 plus 2 is 4   *Multiplying*: 7 times 6 is 53   *Subtracting*: 12 minus 5 is 8
23 plus 12 is 49   13 times 12 is 156   27 minus 13 is 14
13 plus 9 is 21   7 times 8 is 54

A LOT OF   NOT MUCH   NOT MANY (quantities)

Look at these pictures, and study the texts.

*He's got a lot of hair,
but he hasn't got many friends!*

*She hasn't got much hair,
but she's got a lot of wigs!*

① Now complete these sentences with A LOT OF, NOT MUCH or NOT MANY.

    1   There is .... water in Saudi Arabia.
    2   There is .... sand in Saudi Arabia.
    3   There are .... trees in Saudi Arabia.
    4   There are .... books in a library.

FORM

A   Large quantities
We use **a LOT OF** for plurals and uncountables:
    Imelda had a lot of shoes; Ferdinand had a lot of money.
 	
B   Small quantities
We use **NOT MANY** for plurals:
    There aren't many kings and queens in the world.
We use **NOT MUCH** for uncountables:
    You won't get much money for that old car.
 	
Note: Small quantities often means "insufficient", or "not enough".

Good English?

② Look at the underlined parts in these sentences. Three of them are correct and three are wrong.
Tick (✔) the correct ones, and rewrite the wrong ones.

.... 1 He has<u>n't</u> got <u>much time</u>.
.... 2 She has <u>a lot of time.</u>
.... 3 Mr Rockefeller has got <u>much money</u>.
.... 4 There were<u>n't many people</u> at the concert.
.... 5 They bought <u>many coffee</u>.
.... 6 We have <u>much milk</u>.

Mixed Bag

③ Complete each of these sentences twice, using A LOT OF, MUCH or MANY.

1 You haven't got .... chairs,
.... furniture,   the room looks empty.

2 There were .... cars
was .... traffic   on the road this morning.

3 You didn't bring .... suitcases,
.... luggage,   did you?

4 She didn't take .... dollars
.... money   when she went on holiday.

5 I listened to .... songs
.... music   yesterday evening.

More Practice

④ Complete this conversation with A LOT OF, MUCH or MANY, using NOT (............) if necessary.

Example: .... *We've got a lot of plates.* ....

Robert How about cups?
Carol No, we have .... got _____ cups. We'll need to borrow some.
Robert And glasses?
Carol Yes, we have .... got _____ glasses.
Robert How about coke?
Carol No, we have .... got _____ coke; we'll need to get some.
Robert And have we got enough coffee?
Carol We have .... got _____ coffee; can you buy some?
Robert OK, coffee. And how about tea?
Carol Yes, we have .... got _____ tea bags.
Robert Good. And milk for the tea and coffee?
Carol We have .... got _____ milk. You can buy some milk too.
Robert Right. And now food. How about sandwiches?
Carol We have .... got _____ sandwiches; I'm going to make some this afternoon.
Robert Right, I'll help you. How about cakes?
Carol Yes, we have .... got _____ cakes.
Robert And biscuits?
Carol We have .... got _____ biscuits too.
Robert Is that everything?
Carol Yes, I think so. I'll make the sandwiches, and you buy the things we need.

It's a Mad, Mad World!

⑤ Mr Mad is going to Iceland for a holiday! He's taking a lot of bathing costumes, a lot of T-shirts and a lot of sun lotion. Is that right?

No, he should .... take .... bathing costumes or T-shirts,
and he should .... take .... sun lotion.
But he should take .... sweaters and .... warm clothes!

SHE YOU THEM (personal pronouns)

Look at the picture, and study the texts.

He can see her, but she can't see him.

"Yes, I can see you."

They can see him,
but he can't see them.

"You can't see us!"

"Can you see me?"

① Now complete the sentences.

"Look at this photo of John and Mary."
"Which is which?"
"This is .... (he/his/him) and this is .... (she/her). And can you see the dogs?"
"Yes, I can see .... (they/their/them)."
"And here's a picture of .... (you/your) and .... (I/my/me)!"

② Complete this table with the words from the box.

us	they	him
I	her	it	you

	Singular	Singular/plural	Plural
1st person	.... me		we ....
2nd person		you	
3rd person	he		
	she		.... them
	.... it		

Good English?

③ Look at the <u>underlined</u> parts of these sentences. Five of them are correct and four are wrong.
Tick (✓) the correct ones, and rewrite the wrong ones.

....	1	"What do you think of Mary?" "I like <u>her</u>."
....	2	"Where is Robert?" "<u>She</u> is here."
....	3	Are <u>you</u> going by bus?" "No, John is taking <u>we</u>."
....	4	"Are <u>you</u> all well?" "Yes, <u>I</u> are, thank you."
....	5	"What are the girls eating for lunch?" "<u>I</u> am making <u>them</u> a sandwich."
....	6	"Where are the boys?" "<u>He</u> are in the bedroom."

Boys and Girls

④ Look at these pictures, and complete the sentences with I, SHE, HIM, etc.

.... likes .... , but .... doesn't like ....

.... like .... , but .... doesn't like ....

.... likes .... , but .... doesn't like ....

.... like .... , but .... doesn't like ....

.... likes .... , AND .... LIKES .... !

Which Pronoun?

⑤ Choose the correct alternative.

1 I / Me } go to school with { them. / they.

2 He / Him } can play tennis with { she. / her.

3 Come with { we / us } tomorrow.

4 I saw { him / she } yesterday.

5 We / Us } like { they / you } very much.

6 It / He } is a nice day.

7 Him / He } saw { us / we } yesterday.

8 Where are { them / they } going?

9 Ask { him / he } the way.

10 Them / They } are waiting for { we. / you.

11 Us / We } are leaving tonight with { them. / they.

12 I spoke to { her / she } in the office.

⑥ Match these questions and answers.

1 "Where are Robert and Susan?" ....   A "Yes, she is; they are all in the kitchen."
2 "Is Dennis with Victoria?" ....   B "I'm doing this exercise!"
3 "Is Carol with them?" ....   C "They went out to the cinema."
4 "Can you and Fred come with us?" ....   D "Yes, we can; we're free."
5 "And what are you doing?" ....   E "Yes, he's with her."

56

MY YOUR HIS HER THEIR (possessive adjectives)

Look at these pictures, and study the texts.

This is my coat,
and this is your sweater.

"Are these her trainers?"
"No, they're his trainers; look at the size!"

"Aaaagh! Where's our car?"

"Look, their car has gone!"

① Complete these sentences with MY, YOUR, HIS, HER, etc.

1   John dropped .... wallet at the bus stop. But two women with .... children saw him, and said, "Excuse me, you've dropped .... wallet." "Oh, is that .... wallet?" he said. "Thank you very much!"

2   Dennis said to Victoria, "............. children are very good today. Why is that?" Victoria said, "Carol passed .... driving test today; she's very pleased."

USE
We say my hand, my head, etc: I cut my finger. (Not: ✗ I cut the finger.)

FORM

Complete this table:

	Personal pronouns		Possessive adjectives
	Subject	Object	
Singular	I	ME	MY (sister)
	....	HIM	....
	SHE	....	....
Singular/plural	....	YOU	....
Plural	WE	....	....
	THEY	....	....

Good English?

② Look at the underlined words in these sentences. Four of them are correct and four are wrong. Tick (✓) the correct ones, and rewrite the wrong ones.

.... 1   Fred hit his finger with her dad's hammer.
.... 2   Carol washed his face and combed the hair.
.... 3   "Where are your books?" "In my bag."
.... 4   My friend Peter came to visit me with her sister.

Famous People – Including You!

③ Complete these sentences with MY, HIS, HER, THEIR or YOUR and the names from the box.

Example: A famous French painter called Van Gogh

What is ..*his*...... first name? *Vincent*.

Robert	Marie
Brigitte	Indira
Kevin	Pierre
William	?(you)?

1 A famous Indian politician called Ghandi
What is .... first name? ....

2 Two famous scientists called Curie.
What are .... first names? .... and ....

3 A famous English writer called Shakespeare
What is .... first name? ....

4 A famous French actress called Bardot
What is .... first name? ....

5 A famous American actor called Kostner
What is .... first name? ....

6 A famous actor called Redford
What is .... first name? ....

7 A famous student of English: YOU!
What is .... first name?   .... first name is .... !

My Brothers and Sisters

④ Complete the sentence below about "my brothers and sisters, and myself", using words from the box.

me	my	we	us
him	his	you	your
her	her	them	their

I have four brothers and sisters: a boy, a girl and twins (the twins are boys). We all live together.

1 We have three bedrooms; one for .... sister, one for the twins, and one for .... brother and ....

2 .... sister's bedroom is a mess; .... is a very untidy girl, and leaves .... clothes on the floor. .... mother often tells .... to tidy her room.

3 .... brother and .... are untidy too; .... leave .... things all over the house, and .... father tells .... to be tidier.

4 But the twins are very tidy; .... always put .... things away in .... room. Nobody ever says anything to .... !

5 .... parents are not very tidy either. .... father leaves his tools in the kitchen, and .... mother leaves .... sweaters in the living room. .... are a messy family (except for the twins; .... are tidy).

6 And now how about you? Do .... put .... clothes away and keep .... room tidy? Do .... family tell .... to put your things away?

'S   S'   OF   (possessive)

Look at these pictures, and study the texts.

This is Carol's coat, and
these are Robert's shoes.

That is the boys' school,
and this is the women's college.

① Now complete these phrases with 's or '.

... the baby............ bed	... the cat............ dinner
... my uncle............ car	... the girls............ school
... a dogs............ home	... the players............ boots
... the men............ bathroom	... the children............ room

Look at the pictures, and study the texts.

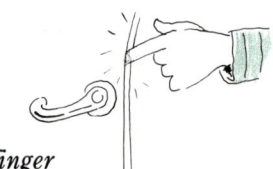

Robert's finger
the door of the car

the girls' feet
the bottom of the bed

② Who do the bicycle, leg, etc., "belong" to? Do they "belong" to living things (L) or objects (O)?

.... Fred's bicycle	.... the leg of the table
.... the engine of my car	.... the dog's collar
.... an ants' nest	.... the back wheel of his bicycle

USE
We put the "owner" first, with **'s** or **s'**, when the "owner" is a person (or an animal):
This is John's car.   It's the twins' bedroom. It's the cat's supper.
We put the "owner" second, with **of the**, when the "owner" is a thing:
The height of the building.

FORM		
	"Owner" first	**"Owner"** second
Singular "owner"	Robert's car	the key of the door
Plural "owner": regular	the boys' school	the age of the buildings
irregular	the men's shoes	

Good English?

③ Look at the <u>underlined</u> parts of these sentences. Three of them are correct, and three are wrong. Tick (✓) the correct ones, and rewrite the wrong ones.

.... 1 He opened <u>the house's door</u> and went in.
.... 2 I want to buy <u>a man's overcoat</u> please.
.... 3 <u>The boys' sweaters</u> are over there, in the corner.
.... 4 Can I see <u>some blouses of women</u>, please?
.... 5 <u>The roof of the house</u> is on fire!
.... 6 Here are <u>shoes' John</u>.

Mixed Bag

④ Now write these out correctly, using 'S, S', or OF. (Be careful you put the words in the correct order!)

John	car	....
the house	roof	....
the men	trousers	....
the tree	leaves	....
the kitchen	door	....
the horse	tail	....
my car	back door	....
Mr Smith	new suit	....
Mary	suitcase	....
the next train	the time	....
the students	work	....
the teacher	comments	....

⑤ Write out these sentences, using 'S, S', ', OF and THE.

1 (John/coat) Where is .... ?
2 (this suitcase/the handle) .... is broken.
3 (Segovia/pupils) They were ....
4 (this substance/the name) .... is Radium.
5 (girls/clothes) They sell .... here.
6 (the game/the second half) .... was very exciting.
7 (his parents/permission) He asked for ....
8 (the parcel/the size) .... affects the cost of postage.
9 (his grandmother/glasses) Fred sat on ....
10 (this pot/the lid) Where is .... ?
11 (teachers/room) You'll probably find Mr Turner in the ....
12 (the place/the size) When I went to the Grand Canyon, ... amazed me.
13 (Fred/room) .... is a terrible mess!
14 (room/door) Can you leave .... open, please?
15 (women/shoes) I am looking for a shop that sells ....
16 (the policeman/helmet) While he was arresting the thief, ... fell off.

MIXED EXERCISES (units 49 - 57)

Here are four exercises which use all the articles, pronouns and possessives practised in Units 49 - 57.

Articles etc.	*Personal pronouns/adjectives*			*Possessives*
a	I	me	my	's
the	you	you	your	s'
some	he/she/it	him/her/it	his/her/its	of the
any	we	us	our	
not many	they	them	their	
not much				
a lot of				

① Choose the right word in each sentence.

1   Peter can't find [his / me / you] shoes.

2   [Us / Our / We] coats are in the cupboard.

3   They left [them / they / their] books in the office.

4   "Where are [your / you / them] shoes?"

5   "We left [they / them / their] in the garden."

6   [I / He / Us] don't know the way home.

7   She took [me / her / she] car to the garage.

8   [My / Me / Us] aunt took [we / our / us] to the cinema.

9   [She / He / I] is a big boy.

10   "Can you tell [me / my / I] the time, please?"

11   [Them / Their / They] are late again.

12   "Where is [me / my / I] bicycle?"

13   [We / Our / Us] are waiting for Brian.

14   "I asked [his / him / he] the time, but he didn't know."

15   [She / He / I] is a nice girl, don't you think?

16   "Can [your / you / her] help me?"

17   "That man is [his / her / him] husband, I think."

18   "They asked [you / your / his] to go to the cinema with them."

19   [We / I / You] am not ready for you.

20   I ask [he / his / him] to help [I / me / my].

② Complete these sentences with 'S, S' or OF THE, and underline the "owner".

Example: Have you met *Mary's* dad?

1 I think this is John............. coat.
2 I left my bicycle at the corner............. street.
3 The roof .... house is flat.
4 The three boy............. coats were lying in a pile on the floor.
5 Where are the children............. shoes?

6 He was standing at the side .... road.
7 Can you open the door .... car?
8 The traveller.............. waiting room is over there.
9 I was lying in bed, listening to the sound .... sea.
10 Austria is a walker............. paradise.

11 He could read a book by the light .... moon.
12 "The Women .... Room" is a famous novel by Marilyn French.
13 They walked to the top .... hill together.
14 The employee .... canteen is upstairs; the food is very good.

③ Complete these sentences with ME etc., MY etc., or 'S etc.
There are sometimes several possibilities.

1 Come and have tea with .... at .... house tomorrow.
2 "*The Name* .... *Rose*" is Umberto Eco .... best book.
3 Have .... seen this film? .... went together last night.
4 The two sisters .... houses were both quite small.
5 "............. husband and I are at home; .... are looking forward to meeting you.

6 There are two trees at the end .... garden.
7 Here are the twins .... sweaters. And where are .... shoes?
8 "We're waiting for you; call .... when .... are ready."
9 What is your sister .... name?

④ Complete these with A, THE, SOME, ANY, NOT MANY, NOT MUCH or A LOT OF.

1 I bought .... sweater and .... underwear, but I didn't buy .... shirt. But .... sweater was too small, so I went back to .... shop and changed it.
2 There are .... people in Iceland; it has a very small population. But it's a big island, and there is .... space.
3 There is .... sand in Saudi Arabia, but there is .... grass. There isn't .... natural lake in Saudi Arabia.
4 "What would you like for lunch?"
"I'd like .... cheese, ... tomato, ... lettuce, and .... bread, please."
"Would you like .... fruit?"
"No, I wouldn't like .... fruit, thank you."
5 "I haven't got .... money, but I've got .... spare time. Do you want .... help?"
"Thank you; I've got .... work to do."
6 "What is .... time?"
"I don't know. I haven't got .... watch."

THIS   THAT   THESE   THOSE

Look at these pictures, and study the texts.

"What's this here?"
"It's a mummy."
"And what are these?"
"They're gold coins.
And these are bracelets,
and this is a ring."

"What's that over there?"
"It's a rhino."
"And what are those?"
"They're hippos.
And those are flamingoes,
and that's an elephant."
"Yes, I know that!"

① Complete this passage with THIS, THESE, THAT or THOSE.

"Can you put ....flowers in .... vase over there?
Oh, and .... books; can you put them in .... bookcase?"

USE

For persons/objects which are near the speaker:
    THIS/THESE
For persons/objects which are far from (not near) the speaker:
    THAT/THOSE

The object may be near/far in **time**...
    At this moment, everyone is ready to go.   (NOW)
    At that time, no one was ready.   (THEN)

The object may be near/far in **space**...
    This is a good place to sit.   (NEAR)
    That place we went to was nice.   (FAR)

FORM

	Near	**Distant**
Singular	this	that
Plural	these	those

These words can be   a) pronouns: This is a comfortable chair
                 b) adjectives: This chair is comfortable.

Good English?

② Look at the underlined parts of these sentences. Three or them are correct and three are wrong. Tick (✔) the correct ones, and rewrite the wrong ones.

.............1   What is <u>these</u>? It's a picture of a rhino.
.............2   Who are <u>those</u> girls? They're my cousins, Sue and Liz.
.............3   <u>That</u> pictures are very beautiful.
.............4   I enjoyed <u>these</u> book very much.
.............5   <u>This</u> steak is delicious.
.............6   Where is John? <u>That</u>'s John, over there.

A New Girl: Her First Day At School

③ Complete the sentences using THIS or THESE.

Come into this room, and let me explain all these things to you.
.... is your room, and .... are your roomates. .... is your bed, and .... drawers are for your clothes. .... is where you put your books, and .... hangars are for you.

④ Complete the sentences using THAT or THOSE.

Look at the building over there and those fields.
.... is the main school, and .... are the playing fields. .... rooms on the ground floor are the classrooms,and .... building there is the gym. .... are some of the teachers over there, and .... is the head teacher.

On Safari

⑤ Look at the picture of a safari, and complete the dialogue using THIS, THAT, THESE or THOSE.

"Can you see .... animal,
between the trees? It's a tiger."
"And what is .... ?"
"Where?"
"Over there."
"Oh, ... 's a spider monkey."
"There aren't many of .... left in the world."
"And what's .... here, on the truck?"
"It's an anteater, and .... are toucans."

BIG SMALL QUICK SLOW (adjectives)

Look at the picture, and study the texts.

She is a big woman.
She is big.

They are small men.
They are small.

USE
We sometimes use adjectives alone after a verb (e.g. BE):   She is big. (*Not:* ✗ She is a big.)

FORM

We put adjectives before the noun:
    a big woman   (*Not:* ✗ a woman big)
 	
Adjectives do not change from singular to plural:
    two big women (*Not:* ✗ two bigs women)

① Here is a list of adjectives. Put them in the blanks, next to their opposites.

cheap	dear	difficult	fast	good	hot	new	quick
short	small	strong	tall	warm	wet	young	dirty

bad   ....   expensive ⎫ ....
big   .... ⎭
clean   ....   long   ⎫ ....
cold   .... ⎭
cool   .... ⎫ slow
dry   .... ⎭
easy   .... ⎫ old
weak   .... ⎭

Good English?

② Look at the underlined parts of these sentences. Two of them are correct and two are wrong.
Tick (✓) the correct ones, and rewrite the wrong ones.

.... 1 He bought <u>a car very expensive</u> in Rome.
.... 2 Here are <u>three easy exercises</u> for you to do.
.... 3 "Can I have <u>a clean towel</u>, please?"
.... 4 <u>Two youngs women</u> came into the room.

Matching Adjectives And Nouns

③ Match an adjective with a noun, and put them in the right sentence.

Adjectives		Nouns	
busy	beautiful	two actors	six girls
famous	friendly	three nurses	a woman
frightened	happy	a child	a dog

1 .... , Roger Moore and Sean Connery, have both played the part of James Bond.
2 Marilyn Monroe was .... , but she died young.
3 There was .... sitting and crying in the corner of the room.
4 .... were laughing and playing together in the street.
5 .... were running up and down the corridors of the hospital.
6 He jumped up and licked my face, but he didn't bite me; he was ....

Opposites

④ Complete each of these sentences with a pair of OPPOSITES from the completed list in Exercise 1 on the previous page.

1 My house was built in 1846, not 1946! Do you like living in an .... house or a .... one?
2 "This house is .... enough to be healthy, and .... enough to be happy." (old saying)
3 Dennis and Victoria's house has three bedrooms and two bathrooms. Do you think that is a .... house or a .... one?
4 Carol's jacket cost £3 secondhand. Do you think that is .... or .... ?
5 How quickly do you walk? Are you a .... or a .... walker?
6 It was a .... day today, 36 degrees, but last night it was .... and I had to wear an overcoat.
7 A giraffe has a very .... neck, but a hippopotamus's neck is quite ....
8 Do you think mathematics is .... ? No, I think it's a very .... subject, and I always get bad marks.
9 I always put a lot of water in my coffee. I don't like .... coffee; I like it ....

Scrambled Sentences

⑤ You have two things to do: a) put these scrambled sentences in order, and b) make some words PLURAL if necessary. Do not change any verbs.

1 bought/went/shirt/John/Oxford Street/nice/to/some/and
....

2 story/she/me/two/told/funny
....

3 street/man/ran/three/the/across/young
....

4 water/girl/drank/were/they/the/a lot of/thirsty/and
....

5 dinner/businessman/sat/rich/to/several/down
....

6 adventure/me/many/told/they/exciting/their/about
....

7 car/woman/got/red/beautiful/two/in/the
....

OLDER   OLDEST   (comparison of adjectives -1)

'Multilevel English Grammar Programme

Look at these pictures, and study the texts.

Holidays for older people!

The oldest football player in the world

Susan is older than Jack.

① Now complete these sentences with forms of the adjectives in the box.

nice	high		
young	long	strong	

1   "My son is 10 years old."
    "This game is for .... children, from five to eight years."
2   The Matterhorn is the .... mountain in Europe.
3   "My dad's .... than your dad!"
4   The river Rhine is long, but the river Nile is ....
5   "I really like him; he's the .... man I know!"

Look at these two common irregular adjectives.

good	-	better	-	best
bad	-	worse	-	worst

② Use them to complete the sentences, then answer the questions.

1   When I was three I got lost in a big store. It was the .... experience in my life. Can you think of one .... than that?
2   The .... day of my life was the day I left school! Can you think of one .... than that?

FORM

		Comparative	Superlative
young	er	younger (than)	the youngest
fat	+t er	fatter (than	the fattest
nice	-e er	nicer (than)	the nicest
pretty	-y +ier	prettier (than)	the prettiest

Jim is big!   Waldo is bigger (than Jim).   Jumbo is the biggest.

Susan is a pretty girl.   She is prettier than Fran.   She is the pretttiest girl in the office.

Mixed Bag

③ Complete each sentence with the correct form of an adjective from the box, and THAN or THE if necessary.

> large   hot   tall
> young   dry

Example:

Uncle Victor is 5'9" tall, Dennis is 5'11" and Clarence is 6'4". Dennis is ...*taller*... than Uncle Victor and Dennis and Clarence is the ...*tallest*... of the three men.

    1a   Ahmed is 17 and Willy (who is 16) is .... than him.
     b   Ali, who is only 15, is the .... of the three friends.
    2a   A whale is .... than a shark.
     b   The Blue Whale is the world's .... animal.
    3a   Venus has a temperature of 462°C. It is .... planet in the solar system.
     b   Mars has a temperature of –23°C. The earth is .... Mars.
    4a   London is wetter in the winter and .... in the summer.
     b   The Atacama desert in Chile is one of .... places in the world.

④ Complete these sentences with the comparative or the superlative form of the adjective, and THE or THAN if necessary).

   Example: Uncle Victor is the (short) *shortest* of the three men.

    1   Spain is much (big) .... Portugal.
    2   The Nile is (long) .... river in Africa.
    3   A library is usually (quiet) .... a football match!
    4   The Cheetah is (fast) .... animal in the world.
    5   In the northern hemisphere, December is (short) .... month, but in the southern hemisphere it is (long) ....
    6   I think English is (easy) .... to understand .... to speak.
    7   Is Mount Everest (high) .... mountain in the world?
    8   Jane is (old) .... her sisters.
    9   If you want to sleep well, hot chocolate is (good) .... coffee.
   10   This is the (noisy) .... flat in the world, I think.

It's a Mad, Mad World!

⑤ Look at these sentences. Mark them True or False, and rewrite the false sentences.

                                                       T   F

    1   The Mediterranean is smaller than the Caspian Sea.   ☐ ☐
    2   The river Danube is longer than the river Thames.   ☐ ☐
    3   Kilimanjaro is the highest mountain in America.   ☐ ☐
    4   The Pacific is the biggest ocean in the world.   ☐ ☐
    5   Venus is closer to the sun than Mars.   ☐ ☐
    6   The Bay of Bengal is larger than Hudson Bay.   ☐ ☐
    7   The largest glacier in the world is the Breadmore Glacier in Antarctica.   ☐ ☐
    8   I am the cleverest person in this group!   ☐ ☐

MORE/MOST INTERESTING (comparison of adjectives –2)

Look at the picture, and study the texts.

"World of Sport" is more expensive than the other books.
"World of Sport" is the most expensive of the four books.

Your Opinion Of the Four Books

① Complete the statements, using the adjectives in brackets.

1 The book on .... is .... than the book on .... (interesting)
2 The book on .... is .... of all the books. (interesting)
3 The book on .... is .... of all the books. (useful)
4 The book on .... is .... than the book on .... (boring)

	FORM	
	Comparative	**Superlative**
big	bigger (than)	the biggest
interesting	more interesting (than)	the most interesting

Most long adjectives give an *opinion!*
Here are three lists of common longer adjectives:

attractive	comfortable	famous	successful
beautiful	expensive	important	useful
amusing	embarrassing	exciting	interesting
boring	entertaining	frightening	surprising
amused	embarrassed	excited	interested
bored	frightened	surprised	

Good English?

② Look at the underlined parts of these sentences. Three of them are correct and three are wrong.
Tick (✓) the correct ones, and rewrite the wrong ones.

............1 This was <u>the more embarrassing</u> moment in my life.
............2 The film was <u>more entertaining than</u> I expected.
............3 John Smith was <u>the most successful</u> man I knew.
............4 The President was <u>most important</u> person in the room.
............5 She was <u>the beautifullest</u> woman I have ever seen.
............6 As a person, he was <u>more interesting than</u> I expected.

More Practice

③ Put in the comparative form of a suitable adjective, and THAN if necessary.

interesting	comfortable
amusing	modern
expensive	crowded

1 This hotel is cheap. The last one was .... this one .
2 The cinema is always .... on Saturday night.
3 The book was good; it was .... the last one I read.
4 The hotel looks very old; I prefer a .... one.
5 I laughed a lot; the film was .... I expected.
6 An armchair is usually .... an upright chair.

④ Complete these sentences. Use the comparative or the superlative form of the adjective, and MORE, THE MOST, or THAN if necessary.

Example: I think that I am (intelligent) ...*more intelligent than*... my brother!

1 "Star Wars" is .... film I have ever seen. (exciting)
2 "Dracula" was .... book I have ever read. (frightening)
3 A Rolls Royce is a better car than a Mercedes, and it's .... (expensive)
4 A saloon car is .... a sports car. (comfortable)
5 Cats are generally .... dogs. (independent)
6 Dogs are usually .... cats. (affectionate)
7 That's .... painting in this exhibition. (beautiful)
8 But that big picture is .... the small one. (impressive)
9 What would happen if .... woman in the world married the .... man? Would their children be .... and .... other children? (beautiful, intelligent)
   No, they wouldn't. It's .... that. (complicated)

It's a Mad, Mad World!

⑤ Look at the picture, and complete the sentences with a comparative form of one of the words in the box.

frightening
good-looking
amusing
intelligent

1 The gorilla is .... the actor.
2 The giraffe is .... the scientist.
3 The mouse is .... the lion.

MIXED EXERCISES (units 61 – 62)

Here are seven activities to practise the comparative and superlative of adjectives. You will need to use all these "comparing words" with the adjectives.

"Comparing Words"	
-er	-est
more	most
than	the

Nature

① Complete these sentences with adjectives from the box and the "comparing words" above. (One of the adjectives is used twice.)

high	beautiful
big	dry

1   The Atacama desert in Chile is .... place in the world; it never rains there!
2   Lake Superior in North America is .... Lake Victoria in Africa.
3   In fact, Lake Superior is .... lake in the world.
4   The Sacred Valley in Peru is .... valley I have ever seen in my life.
5   Mont Blanc (4,807m) is .... the Matterhorn.

Cities and Countries

② Complete these sentences with adjectives from the box and the "comparing words" above.

important	good	small
large	hot	tall
expensive		

1   .... building in London is the Canary Wharf Tower at 243.8m.
2   Portugal is .... Greece; it's only 92,000 km2, and Greece is 132,000 km2.
3   Madrid is .... Paris in the summer; the temperature is over 40°C.
4   Tokyo is .... London; rents are very high.
5   China has .... population in the world.
6   As a financial centre, London is .... Paris.
7   Theatres in Paris and New York are good, but .... theatres in the world are in London.

People and Their Achievements

③ Make up sentences using one part from each of the three sections, and the "comparing words" above.

1	2000 years ago, Rome was	A	beautiful sight	i	of classical music
2	Pele was	B	fast plane	ii	in the western world
3	The Concorde is	C	great composer	iii	in India
4	The Taj Mahal is	D	important city	iv	in the BA fleet
5	I think Beethoven is	E	good footballer	v	in Brazil

Personal Experiences

④ Complete these sentences with a word from the box, using the "comparing words" at the top of the previous page.

> boring   comfortable   frightened
> embarrassing   entertaining

1   .... moment of Robert's life was when he walked into the ladies lavatory by mistake!
2   When we went to see "Count Dracula", I was .... my sister; she wasn't very frightened at all.
3   I like magazines; they are .... school books!
4   This book on mathematics is horrible; it's .... I have ever read in my whole life.
5   I always sit in the big armchair; it's .... chair in the house.

Films, Books, TV: Better, Best, or Worse, Worst?

⑤ Complete these sentences. On the dotted line, you must put the name of a film (or a book, or a TV programme); on the straight line you must put BETTER, BEST, WORSE or WORST. Use THAN or THE if necessary

1   I thought .... was _____ film I have ever seen.
2   I thought .... was _____ film I have ever seen
3   I thought .... was _____ than ....
4   I thought .... was _____ than ....

Three People

⑥ Compare these people, using the adjectives given.

TALL/SHORT
1   Robert is the .... ; he measures 1m 85.
    Fred is the............ .
    Carol is .... Fred.
FAT/SLIM
2   Fred is .... Carol; he is 36 inches around the waist.
    Carol is .... Robert.
    Carol is .... of the three.

Three Cars

⑦ Look at the information on the cars, and complete the sentences, using an adjective from the box and the "comparing words" above at the top of the previous page.

	Engine	Safety	Comfort	Price
Rolls Horse	✔✔✔	✔✔	✔✔✔	£50,000
Stroller	✔	✔✔✔	✔	£12,000
Cheetah	✔✔	✔	✔✔	£43,000

> safe   powerful   comfortable
> dangerous   expensive

1   The Rolls Horse has a very big engine; it is .... a Stroller.
2   The Stroller has a very good accident record; it is .... of the three cars.
3   At £43,000, the Cheetah is .... the Stroller.
4   The Cheetah is .... the Stroller; it has leather padded seats.
5   The Cheetah is .... of the three cars; it has a bad accident record.

QUICKLY   SLOWLY   WELL (adverbs)

Look at these pictures and study the texts.

They're talking to each other on carphones.

She drives quickly.
She drives her car quickly.
She drives well.

"I'm going home!" she said happily.

He drives slowly.
He drives his car slowly.
He drives badly.

"I've got to work," he said sadly.

① Now you have to look at these pictures, and write out the sentences again, adding an adverb. It must be (a) the right adverb and (b) in the right place.

1   Robert typed the letter. ....
2   Carol sings. ....
3   Robert plays football. ....
4   Fred is running. ....

FORM

A   We often make adverbs from adjectives by adding -ly:

adjective	adverb
bad +ly	badly
slow +ly	slowly
happy -y +ily	happily
Note: good	well

B   Main position in the sentence:

Robert plays [badly] ▼

Robert plays football [badly] ▼

Good English?

② Look at the <u>underlined</u> parts of these sentences. Two of them are correct and two are wrong. Tick (✓) the correct ones, and rewrite the wrong ones.

...............1   Uncle Victor does <u>his work slow.</u>
...............2   Winston can <u>run quickly.</u>
...............3   Carol plays <u>well the piano.</u>
...............4   Dennis cooked <u>the supper badly.</u>

More Practice

③ First, you have to complete each sentence with an adverb in the right place.

QUICKLY   1 Fred did his homework.
SLOWLY   2 Uncle Victor walks; he's very old now.
WELL   3 Carol speaks French, and she likes it.
HAPPILY   4 The children went to the party.
SADLY   5 They said goodbye.

④ Now you have to make adjectives from these adverbs, and put them in the right place in the sentences.

FLUENT   1 Robert speaks German.
CORRECT   2 He can't use the verbs.
CAREFUL   3 Robert was going to see his girl friend Sandra, so he combed his hair and
               left the house.
TENDER   4 "I like you very much," he told his girlfriend.
LOUD   5 "Please do not talk. This is a hospital."
POLITE   6 "I hope you had a very nice day," he said.
RUDE   7 "Go and jump in the lake!" she said.

⑤ Now you have to complete the sentence on the top with an adverb, and the sentence below it with an adjective. Choose a word from the box for each pair of sentences.

> passionately angrily happily
> nervously   confidently

Example: "If you do that, I'll kill you!" he said ....*angrily*....
          He is an ....*angry*.... man.

1   "I'm sure I can do that," she said ....
    She is a .... person.
2   "I love you!" she cried ....
    She is a .... woman.
3   "Today is a wonderful day!" he said ....
    He is a .... man.
4   "I can't cross the road by myself" the child said ....
    He is a .... little boy.

It's a Mad, Mad World!

⑥ Look at these sentences; the adverbs are wrong. Can you move each adverb to the right sentence? The first is done for you.

1   "Go away!!" he shouted politely.   ....*he shouted rudely.*....
2   "I am very pleased with my exam result," he said angrily ....
3   "I don't like this book much" he said passionately   ....
4   "This is the best book in the world!!" he said quietly   ....
5   "I am furious with that man!" she said happily   ....
6   "How kind of you!" she said rudely   ....

ALWAYS OFTEN SOMETIMES NEVER (adverbs of frequency)

Look at these pictures, and study the texts.

Robert always cleans his shoes.

Carol often cleans her shoes but not always.

Fred sometimes cleans his shoes.

Uncle Victor never cleans his shoes.

① Now complete each sentence with a word from the box.

> always   often
> sometimes   never

1   Fred is not interested in the time; he is .... late.
2   Uncle Victor is .... late, but not always; he doesn't care!
3   Carol tries to be early, but she is .... late.
4   Robert is very well organised; he is .... late.

USE

Position In the Sentence
We put these words before the main verb and after the auxiliary verbs:

Carol [often] ↓ works hard.

Fred will [sometimes] ↓ work hard.

Robert is [never] ↓ late.

Robert doesn't [often] ↓ go to the cinema.

Meaning

always	✓	✓	✓	✓	✓	✓	✓	✓	✓	✓	(100%)
often	✓		✓	✓		✓	✓	✓		✓	(about 60–80%)
sometimes		✓		✓		✓			✓		(about 20–60%)
never											(0%)

Good English?

② Look at the <u>underlined</u> parts of these sentences. Two of them are correct and two are wrong.
Tick (✓) the correct ones, and rewrite the wrong ones.

............1   Fred <u>plays sometimes</u> football.
............2   Victoria <u>often goes</u> out on a Saturday evening.
............3   Uncle Victor <u>is always</u> in a good mood.
............4   Robert <u>never has smoked</u>.

What Is the Weather Like?

③ Look at this weather chart, and describe the places, as in the example.

	it rains	it snows	it's sunny	it's cold	it's hot
The Sahara desert	–	–	✔✔✔✔	✔✔	✔✔✔
The Arctic	✔✔	✔✔✔	✔✔	✔✔✔✔	–
Singapore	✔✔	–	✔✔✔	–	✔✔✔✔
London	✔✔	✔✔	✔✔	✔✔	✔✔
Where you live	?	?	?	?	?

Example: ...... *In the Sahara it never rains and it never snows. It is sometimes cold, but it is often hot.* ......

1   In the Arctic ....
2   In Singapore ....
3   In London ....
4   Where I live ....

Jobs: What Do They Do?

④ Look at the information about each job, and complete the sentences.

Jane	*secretary*	uses a computer	✔✔✔
		uses a typewriter	✔✔
John	*English policeman*	wears a helmet	✔✔✔✔
		carries a gun	–
Peter	*doctor*	has treated children with measles	✔✔✔
		has seen a patient with cholera	–
Susan	*manager*	is ready to talk to clients	✔✔✔✔
		has arrived late at the office	✔✔

1   Jane is a .... She .... ,
    and she ....
2   John is a .... He .... ,
    but he ....
3   Peter is a .... He .... ,
    but he ....
4   Susan is a .... She .... ,
    and she ....

Your Eating Habits

⑤ Using words from the box, complete these sentences about what you eat and when you eat it.

always	often
sometimes	never

1   I .... eat cheese for breakfast.
2   I have .... eaten sandwiches for lunch.
3   I have .... eaten a rabbit.
4   Turkey meat is .... on sale in the shops where I live.
5   Mangoes are .... on sale in the shops where I live.
6   .... is/are .... on sale where I live.

MIXED EXERCISES (units 64 – 65)

These adverbs were presented and practised in Units 64-65. The six exercises below give further practice.

Mixed Bag – 1 Adjectives to Adverbs

① Complete these sentences with an adverb similar to the adjective in **bold**.

1   He is a **careful** person; he always speaks ....
2   He is an **angry** man, and he shouted .... at his wife.
3   He is a **good** worker; he does his work ....
4   She's a **happy** girl, and she always smiles ....
5   This work is all **correct**; they've done it ....
6   He is a **polite** person, and treats everybody ....
7   He is a **passionate** person; he does everything ....

Work In an Office

② You have to put the adverb in the right place in the sentence.

1   Sue speaks French.   FLUENTLY
2   She gets to the office in good time.   ALWAYS
3   She has been ill.   NEVER
4   Today, she walked into the office.   CONFIDENTLY
5   She has spent the morning on the phone.   OFTEN
6   She typed the three letters.   CORRECTLY
7   She files her papers in the filing cabinet.   CAREFULLY
8   She has coffee with her friend Helen.   SOMETIMES
9   They drink tea.   NEVER
10   They finish their coffee and go back to work.   QUICKLY

Mixed Bag – 2 Which Adverb?

③ You have to choose from the adverbs in the boxes the one you think best fits the meaning
of the sentence.

| rudely   badly   sadly |
| quickly   politely |

1   He didn't understand computers, and he did the work ....
2   "Excuse me, I wonder if you could help me?" he said ....
3   She ran .... down the street, and in two minutes she was home.
4   "Get out of my way!" he shouted ....
5   "I shall probably never see her again," he said ....

| loudly   well   arrogantly |
| slowly   happily |

6   The old man walked .... up the stairs.
7   "Hello! Can you hear me?" he said ....
8   She did her work .... and her boss congratulated her.
9   "I've just had a pay rise!" she announced ....
10   "There's nothing I can't do!" he told her ....

Mixed Bag – 3 Word Order

④ You must put these words in the right order to make a sentence, making sure the adverb is in the best place.

1 drove/the scene/quickly/the crime/the police/to/of

   ....

2 on Fridays/the movies/to/we/often/go

   ....

3 the door/he/his hand/loudly/hit/with

   ....

4 octopus/seen/never/an/have/I

   ....

5 the guitar/all his life/well/played/he

   ....

6 sometimes/sometimes/win/lose/and/you/you/

   ....

Going To Work

⑤ Look carefully at these sentences; they need an adverb to make better sense. Add the four adverbs from the box in the right places.

always	often
sometimes	never

1 I catch the same train every day; that why I am late for work.
2 Mike catches an early train two or three days a week, and the other days he catches a late train; that's why he is late for work.
3 Susan comes to work by car, but it's a very old car and it doesn't work properly; that why she is late for work.
4 Jimmy cannot get up in the morning; it seems to be impossible for him. That's why he is late for work.

Emotions (A) and Skills (B)

⑥ You have to place these four adverbs in the best places in the two sets of sentences. There is one obvious place for each adverb, but there are other possibilities.

A
passionately	angrily
tenderly	nervously

B
fluently	correctly
carefullly	confidently

A 1 "After what you have done, I never want to see you again!" he shouted.
   2 "But what have I done?" she said.
   Next day they met again; he forgot his anger.
   3 "I shall love you for ever!" he cried. "Can you still love me?"
   4 "Of course I can, silly," she said to him, and kissed him on the cheek.

B 1 He placed the computer in the car because he did not want to break it.
   2 He walked into the meeting, and began to speak in a firm voice.
   3 "You must do this; don't make any mistakes!"
   4 She spoke Russian.

A BOOK   BOOKS   A MAN   MEN   (plurals)

Look at these pictures, and study the texts.

Two old men, their feet and their teeth...

The women and the children...

These women have many knives in their lives.

① Now complete these sentences with the plural of the right word in the box.

1   The .... are all in school today.
2   A thousand .... work here.
3   They say a cat has nine .... ! (But it's not true.)
4   Clean your .... every day. (Twice!)

life	man
tooth	child

FORM

A   Most nouns from their plurals with *-s*, *-es* or *-ies*:

–s		–es		–y +ies	
book	word	class	watch	country	fly
books	words	classes	watches	countries	flies

B   These nouns change a little:

knife	wife	life	leaf	etc.
knives	wives	lives	leaves	

C   These five common nouns are irregular:

man	woman	child	foot	tooth
men	women	children	feet	teeth

Good English?

② Look at the underlined parts of the sentences. Four of them are correct and four are wrong. Tick (✓) the correct ones, and rewrite the wrong ones.

.... 1 A men bought two sandwiches.

.... 2 There are three childs waiting for you.

.... 3 This book is on the lifes of famous women.

.... 4 There were twelve countrys in the Common Market in 1992.

.... 5 Look! His feet are covered in flies!

More Practice

③ Complete these sentences with a word from the box, in the singular or plural.

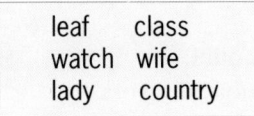

man   woman   child
tooth   foot   knife

1 He jumped into the water .... first.
2 He went to the dentist because he had a bad ....
3 Some .... help their wives in the house.
4 There's a .... on the phone for you; I didn't ask her name."
5 "You put your left .... in, you take your left .... out, you do the hokey cokey and you turn around, that's what it's all about." (Traditional English dance)
6 A .... called Mr Brian Smith came to the house.
7 You should clean your .... twice a day.
8 "How old are those .... ?"
   "They're about 11 or 12 years old, I think."
9 The three .... had their babies on the same day.
10 A .... about six years old ran in front of the car.
11 "Please put the .... and forks out on the table for four people."

④ Complete these sentences with a word from the box, in the singular or plural.

leaf   class
watch   wife
lady   country

1 Two .... and two gentlemen were having tea.
2 Tea is made from the .... of a plant.
3 "What's the time?"
   "I'm sorry, I haven't got a ...."
4 I've got a French .... this evening.
5 .... and husbands must learn to be friends.
6 We sell clocks and ....
7 .... at the Edgar English Language School are between 9 am and 1 pm, Monday to Friday.
8 "Can you and your .... come to dinner tonight at 7.30?"
   "Sorry. We're leaving the ...., this afternoon."
9 The cleaning .... comes to the house at 9 am on Mondays.
10 Look! The first green .... I have seen this Spring!

MUSIC and SONGS (countable and uncountable)

Look at these pictures, and study the texts.

Can you count sheep?

Can you count music?
Can you count water?

① Complete these with A, a number (2, 7, etc.) or nothing.

1 There are .... bags and .... suitcase in the car.

2 You can buy .... furniture in any furniture store, but you'll need .... money to pay for it!

3 John wants .... job; he needs .... work.
He hasn't got .... profession.

USE

A   *singular*   a tree
       plural   three trees   trees
       uncountable   music
 	
 B   You can count most things:
       a boy   100 women   2 cities   5 books   etc.
 	
 There are some things you cannot count:
       music   (*Not:* ✗ a music   *Not:* ✗ 3 musics)   *But:* some music
       water   (*Not:* ✗ a water   *Not:* ✗ 5 waters)   *But:* some water
 	
 C   Here is a selection of words you (usually!) cannot count:
       food   butter   bread   cheese   milk   work   money   work
       air   water   fire   music   clothing   furniture   transport   permission
 	
 Here is a selection of words which you cannot count in English
 (in some languages you <u>can</u> count them):
       accommodation   luggage   information   news   traffic   weather

② Match the words on the left with the words on the right. The first pair is done for you.

a flat   5 dollars   a job   2 songs   a table   a profession   a pound (£)   4 chairs   3 bags   6 suitcases   a symphony   3 hotel rooms

music   *2 songs*   *a symphony*
work   ....
luggage   ....
furniture   ....
money   ....
accommodation   ....

More Practice

③ Complete these sentences with A, TWO (or another number) or nothing.

1   I like a nice cup of tea, but I also like .... water.
2   The family have .... houses and .... flat.
3   Simon doesn't like .... work very much, and he hasn't got .... job.
4   He's buying .... shirts and .... jacket.
5   The house is finished; now it needs .... furniture.
6   Mr Wiseman is .... dentist.
7   "............. money is the root of all evil."
8   Dogs have .... legs, and spiders have .... legs.
9   A managing director needs .... information about his company.
10 It's hard to find .... accommodation in London.

④ Choose the correct word from the two given in brackets.

1   It's difficult to find a .... these days. (work/job)
2   Ladies' .... is sold here. (clothing/skirts)
3   We need a .... to go to the airport. (transport/car)
4   What beautiful .... ! (furniture/chair)
5   That'll cost you ten .... (dollars/money)

⑤ Complete each sentence using a word from the box

accommodation   furniture   luggage   information
news   permission   traffic   weather   work

1   I think the new house is pretty, but it needs ....
2   If you want to stay out late, you'll need .... from your parents.
3   We are going to Paris for the weekend, and we need .... Do you know a cheap hotel?
4   We have a lot of clothes, but the airline only lets you take 20 kilos of ....
5   Before I buy anything, I always ask for .... about it.
6   If you haven't got any money, you must look for ....
7   .... on the front pages of newspapers is always bad.
8   In big cities .... moves slowly.
9   .... forecasts are usually wrong; they say it will rain, and the sun shines!

It's a Mad, Mad World!

⑥ Mr Mad is in a mess! Can you help him by sorting out all the items in the boxes?

Mr Mad's trip to a rented house on the moon.

Right, we need some luggage.

> Yes sir, I have a chair and ten pounds .

And we need accommodation.

> Yes sir, I have a suitcase and a hotel room .

And we need furniture.

> Yes, sir I have a flat and a folding bed .

And we need money.

> Yes sir, I have travellers' cheques and a briefcase .

WHO   WHAT   WHERE (question words – 1)

Look at these pictures, and study the texts.

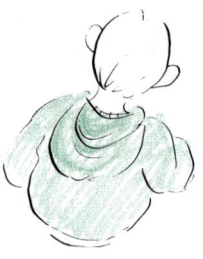

"Who is that?"   *"It's Fred."*
"What is he carrying?"   *"A jumbo sandwich."*
"Where is he going?"   *"Upstairs, to his room."*

① Now complete each sentence with WHO, WHAT or WHERE.

1   .... are you going today?
2   .... are you doing tomorrow?
3   .... are you talking to?
4   .... is the time, please?

USE

A   We use **WHO** for people: B   We use **WHAT** for things:
Who is he?   What is that?
Who are you going with?   What are you doing?

C   We use **WHERE** for place and direction:
Where do you live?
Where are you going?

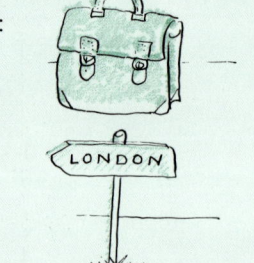

FORM

Word order:

| Where | are you going? |
You are going | to Spain |.

| What | are you doing? |
You are doing | Unit 69 |.

| Who | are you going with? |
You are going with | Richard |

| Who | were you talking with? |
You were talking with | Peter |

Good English?

② Two of these questions are right and two are wrong. Tick (✓) the correct ones, and rewrite
the wrong ones.

............1   <u>What he is doing?</u> Writing letters.
............2   <u>Who is that?</u> It's my brother.
............3   <u>Where you going?</u> Home.
............4   <u>Who are you going out with</u> tomorrow? My brother.

More Practice

③ Match these questions to the answers.

1	Where is Sally?	A	She's gone to the Chinese takeaway.
2	Who is that, talking to Robert?	B	I'm learning English.
3	What is Uncle Victor doing?	C	It's an old friend from university.
4	Where is Carol?	D	She's up a tree in the garden.
5	What are you doing?	E	He's reading the newspaper.

④ Complete these sentences with WHO, WHAT or WHERE.

1 "............ is this bus going, please?"   "To Chigwell."
2 "............ is going to drive it?"   "I am, Miss."
3 "............ time does it leave?"   "When it's full."
4 "............ can I sit?"   "On the floor."
5 "............ is this on the floor?"   "It's oil, Miss."
6 "............ is that man sitting under the tree?"   "He's the regular driver of the bus, Miss."

⑤ Write questions for these answers, as in the example.

Example: ......*Where is he?*................................. He's in the garden.

1 .... (Auntie Mabel) .... ? She's watering the plants.
2 .... (Winston) .... ? He's at the bottom of the tree.
3 .... ? That's Uncle Victor, sitting in the deckchair.
4 .... (Uncle Victor) ....? He's reading the newspaper.
5 .... (Sally) .... ? She's up the tree, looking at Winston.

It's a Mad, Mad World: The Real Truth In the Palace!

⑥ Are the answers to the questions correct? If not, correct them.

"*Who is that, sitting on the throne?*"   "*It's the King.*"
"*What is that, at his feet?*"   "*It's his dog.*"
"*Where is the Queen?*"   "*She's sitting on the small throne.*"
"*What is the King holding in his hand?*"   "*It's an orb.*"
"*Who is the man talking to the King?*"   "*It's the prime minister.*"
"*Where is the fool?*"   "*Sitting on the ground.*"

WHEN HOW WHY BECAUSE

(question words – 2, and word order in questions)

Look at the picture, and study the texts.

"When did you go to Canada?"   *"In 1955."*
"How did you go?"   *"I went by ship."*
"Why did you go?"   *"Because I wanted adventure."*

① Now complete these sentences with WHEN, HOW, WHY or BECAUSE.

1   .... did Robert get in touch with Conran's?
     .... he wanted a job.
2   .... did he write? Last month.
3   .... did he get in touch with them? He telephoned them.

USE
A   **WHEN** did you go?   At six o'clock/on Wednesday in March/in 1992.
B   **HOW** did you go?   By bus/by train/on foot. C   **HOW** did you do that?   With a knife/with my hands.
D   **WHY** did you go?   **BECAUSE** I wanted to go!

FORM

Word order for questions:
He went yesterday.   He went by bus
          When did he go?   How did he go ?
He is going to Spain.   He went to Spain because he wanted to.
          Where is he going?   Why did he go to Spain?

Good English?

② In these sentences, four of the <u>underlined</u> parts are correct, and four are wrong. Tick (✓) the correct ones, and rewrite the wrong ones.

............1   <u>Why did the chicken cross</u> the road?
....   <u>Because he want</u> to get to the other side.
............2   <u>Where you going?</u> Home.
............3   <u>When is the plane leaving?</u> At 7.45.
............4   <u>Why he did come</u> to see you?
....   <u>Because he wanted</u> my help.
............5   <u>Where is my coat?</u> It's on that chair.
............6   <u>When is he going?</u> To Geneva.

More Practice

③ Match the questions and the answers.

1	Why are you going to the conference?	A	In the Town Hall.
2	Where is the conference taking place?	B	I think I'll go by car.
3	When is the conference starting?	C	Well, I need a change from the office!
4	How are you getting to Manchester?	D	On Wednesday evening.

Word Order

④ Put these sentences in the right order. (Don't forget capital letters and punctuation!)

1 tonight/Victoria/where/going/is

....

2 she/the concert/to go/does/why/want/to

....

3 Beethoven's/because/likes/music/she

....

4 you/to/do/the answer/know/this question/how

....

5 when/the concert/start/does

....

Questions For Answers

⑤ Make questions for these answers.

The questions are all about Fred; he broke a window at home!

1 .... ? He broke the window yesterday.
2 .... ? He was playing football in the garden.
3 .... ? His mother saw the broken window when she came
   home from work.
4 .... ? No, she didn't get angry.
5 .... ? Because she realised it was an accident.
6 .... ? Fred repaired the window temporarily with a sheet
   of plastic.

It's a Mad, Mad World!

⑥ Sort out this mad conversation (if you can!).

"How are you?" "It's six o'clock."
"Certainly not! He's leaving tonight, on the morning plane."
"Where's he going?" "Because he thinks the world is mad."
"I'm terribly ill." "What time is it?"
"When is he leaving, tomorrow?"
"And why is he doing that?"
"To the moon, of course! Where else?"

HOW OLD....?   WHAT COLOUR.....?   WHAT.......LIKE?
(question words – 3)

Look at the picture, and study the texts.

"How old is Carol?"
"She's eighteen."
"What colour are her eyes?"
"They're green."
"How tall is she?"
"She's 1m 55."

"How big is her room?"
"It's 4m by 3m."

"What is Carol like?"
"She's intelligent.
She's adventurous.
She sometimes forgets things."

① Now complete these questions.

1	.... Fred?	He's 1m 36.
2	.... ?	He's naughty but nice.
3	.... ?	He's thirteen.
4	.... ?	They're brown.

FORM

A **HOW** + adjectives: How big ... ?   B **WHAT** + nouns: What colour ... ?
                                                   How old ... ?   What size ....?

C **WHAT** ... **LIKE?** (*Not*: ✗ **HOW**) to ask for descriptions of people, places and things:
   What is Salzburg like? It's a beautiful old city.
   What is Robert like? He's a serious, hardworking young man.
   What's that book like? It's good.

Good English?

② Look at the <u>underlined</u> parts of these sentences. Three of them are correct and three are wrong.
Tick (✓) the correct ones, and rewrite the wrong ones.

.... 1   "<u>What colour is</u> a stop light?" "It's red."
.... 2   "<u>What is like Susan?</u> "She is very nice."
.... 3   "<u>How old is the baby?</u>" "She's six months."
.... 4   "<u>How is</u> Susan?" "She's a tall girl."
.... 5   "<u>How big your room is?</u>" "It's about 4m by 5m."
.... 6   "<u>How old is Robert?</u>" "He is 24."

Mixed Bag

③ Here are some descriptions of people and places. Write appropriate questions using an item from the box on the previous page to match the descriptions.

A   *A House*

1.. the house?

It has 3 bedrooms.

2.. ?

It's 40 years old.

3.. the front door?

It's red.

4.. ?

It's an attractive house.

B   *Robert*

1.. ?

They're blue.

2.. ?

He's well organised.

3.. ?

He's 26 years old.

4.. ?

He's 1m 80.

C   *Hampton, the town where they live*

1.. the town?

It has about 10,000 inhabitants.

2.. ?

It's a pretty place.

3.. ?

Several hundred years old.

D   *Victoria*

1.. ?

They're brown.

2.. ?

She's 48 years old.

3.. ?

She's very efficient.

4.. ?

She's 1m 63.

E   *Fred's school*

1.. ?

It has about 600 students.

2.. ?

Not very old; it opened in 1956.

3.. ?

It's a good school, I think.

YES, I HAVE   NO, HE WASN'T

Look at these pictures, and study the texts.

"Is that a boy?"
"Yes, it is."

"Are you sure?"
"Oh, no, it isn't; it's a girl!"

"Is there room for a little one?"
"Yes, there is."

"No, there isn't!"

"Did you break the window?"
"No, I didn't."

"Yes, he did!"

① Answer these questions. (There can always be two answers.)

1   Can you speak French? ....
2   Did Carol go with you to the shops? ....
3   Does Robert like classical music? ....
4   Is there a TV station in your town? ....

USE

When we answer a question, we usually give a short answer:
Examples: Do you often go to the movies? Yes.
                                  Yes, I do.
 	
What time is it? Seven o'clock.
                It's seven o'clock.

FORM
Can you play the violin?   Yes, I can.   No, I can't. Did you play?   Yes, I did.   No, I didn't. Do you play often?   Yes, I do.   No, I don't. Have you played today?   Yes, I have.   No, I haven't. Is there a good orchestra in your town?   Yes, there is.   No, there isn't etc.

Good English?

② Two of these short answers are correct and two are wrong. Tick (✓) the correct ones, and rewrite the wrong ones.

.... 1 Did you like the film? <u>Yes, I have.</u>
.... 2 Is that your bike? <u>No, it isn't.</u>
.... 3 Will she be here at six? <u>Yes, she will.</u>
.... 4 Does he speak German? <u>No, he don't.</u>

Victoria Is Asking Questions

③ Victoria, a mother, is asking her children questions. There are two possible answers to each question. Give them both, as in the example.

Example: "Did you go to school yesterday, Fred?"

.......*Yes, I did.*....................*No, I didn't.*.........

1 "Will you be coming home for supper tonight, Robert?"

....

2 "Fred, have you washed the dishes?"

....

3 "Are you doing your homework, Carol?

....

4 "Did Dennis go to his club meeting?"

....

5 "Has the dog had his supper?"

....

6 "Can you understand your homework, Fred?"

....

7 "Is your Uncle Victor coming home for supper tonight?"

....

General Knowledge

④ Answers these questions. Yes or No?

1   Did Napoleon invade Russia?   ....
2   Will the new millenium start on January 1st 2000?   ....
3   Has Costa Rica got an army?   ....
4   Does the Iron Curtain still exist?   ....
5   Is Mexico in North America?   ....
6   Did the First World War start in 1916?   ....
7   Is it possible to have "English nationality"?   ....
8   Can people from your country work in Great Britain?   ....
9   Did the Romans speak Greek?   ....
10 Have most Japanese got black hair?   ....

It's a Mad, Mad World!

⑤ Look at the picture, and answer the questions.

1   Does the driver know how to drive?   4   Has the bus got good tyres?
2   Is there plenty of room in the bus?   5   Are you glad you're not on the bus?
3   Are they going to crash?

IS HE?   DIDN'T YOU? (question tags)

Look at these pictures, and study the texts.

You can carry that, can't you?

You can't carry that, can you?

The old man'll be late, right?

We are expecting Mr Smith later, aren't we?

① Complete these sentences with phrases from the box.

1   They arrived at six, ... ?
2   She won't come tonight, ... ?
3   John hasn't finished yet, ... ?
4   He's OK, ... ?

isn't he	didn't they
has he	will she

USE

We use question tags when we are not sure of something:
   You are 20 years old, aren't you?
   (I think you are 20 years old, but I am not sure.)

Note: Among friends, we often use informal question tags which don't change: right? OK?

FORM

This is similar to *short* answers (see Unit 72):

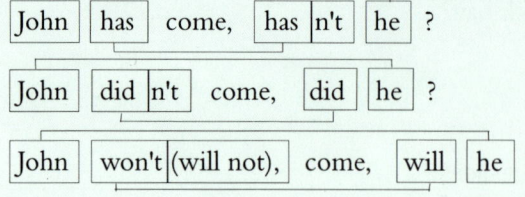

Good English?

② Look at the <u>underlined</u> question tags in these six sentences. Three of them are right and three are wrong.
Tick (✔) the correct ones, and rewrite the wrong ones.

.... 1   Robert and Fred are brothers, <u>don't they</u>?
.... 2   He won't be ready in time, <u>will he</u>?
.... 3   I have passed the test, <u>haven't I</u>?
.... 4   Sue comes every day, <u>isn't she</u>?
.... 5   You can't speak Russian, <u>can you</u>?
.... 6   Carol left early this morning, <u>does she</u>?

A Journey

③ Look at this picture of a couple setting off in the car with their two children; they want to be sure they haven't forgotten anything. Complete the spaces with question tags and short answers (YES, I DID etc.).

		Short Answers
A	*The Car*	
	You filled up with petrol, ... ?	....
	We have got enough water, ... ?	....
	The suitcase won't fall off, ... ?	....
	The tyres are all right, ... ?	....
	You checked the oil, ... ?	....
B	*The Children*	
	The children have brought their toys, ... ?	....
	Peter is wearing his glasses, ... ?	....
	They won't be cold, ... ?	....
	They both went to the bathroom, ... ?	....
	Susan washed her face, ... ?	....
C	*The Journey*	
	We'll be there in about three hours, ... ?	....
	The hotel is booked, ... ?	....
	You know the way, ... ?	....
	The road isn't dangerous, ... ?	....
	You've driven there before, ... ?	....
D	*The Arrival*	
	This is the hotel, ... ?	....
	We didn't take long, ... ?	....
	The rooms won't be cold, ... ?	....
	We haven't been here before, ... ?	....
	We are going to enjoy ourselves, ... ?	....

Overheard In a Cocktail Party

④ Complete these remarks with question tags, then join the question and reply. One joining is done for you.

1 "That hairstyle is crazy, ...*D*...... ?"   A "What does he see in her?"
2 "She went to Paris with her boyfriend, ... ?"   B "Don't say that! That's my mother and my aunt!"
3 "He's not going to talk to her, ... ?"
4 "Those two look absolutely dreadful, ... ?"   C "It wasn't Paris; it was Madrid."
      D "Yes, she looks like a bowl of fruit."

MIXED EXERCISES (units 69 - 73)

Here are two exercises which practise all the words and phrases presented in Units 69 - 73.

who?	what?	how?	Yes, I have (etc.)
where?	what size?	how old?	No, he isn't (etc.)
when?	what colour?	how big?	aren't you? (etc.)
why?	what time?	how tall?	is she? (etc.)
because	what ... like?		

Kate Has a New Boyfriend

① Read this conversation and fill in the blanks. Use the best word or phrase from the box. Sometimes there is more than one possible answer.

1 .... is your new boyfriend .... ?
  He's tall, and he's very nice; well, I think he is!

2 .... is he?
  He's 1m 80.

3 Oh, that's quite tall, ... ?
  Yes, ...

4 And is he good looking?
  Yes, ...

5 .... did you meet him?
  I met him at a dance in the village hall.

6 .... was that?
  It was about six weeks ago.

7 And do you want to marry him?
  Yes, ... , I think.

8 .... ?
  .... he's nice, and we get on well together.

9 .... are his eyes?
  They're brown, and they're quite big.

10 .... is he?
  He was 25 yesterday.

11 Oh! .... did you buy for his birthday?
  I bought him a shirt, but it was the wrong size!

12 .... did you buy?
  I bought a 16 neck, and he takes 15.

13 .... does his father do?
  He's a hospital manager.

14 .... are you meeting him?
  Tomorrow, we're having tea, but I don't want to go!

15 .... not? You're not frightened, ... ?
  Yes, ... , very much!

16 Wait a minute; you're a nice-looking girl, ... ?
  Yes, ... , I suppose.

17 And you went to a good university, ... ?
  Yes, ...

18 And you've got a good job, ... ?
  Yes, ...

19 So, ... are you frightened?
  I don't know!.

An Interview For a Job

② Read this conversation and fill in the blanks. Use the best word or phrase from the ones in the box at the top of the previous page. Sometimes there is more than one possible answer.

1 Good morning, I'm Jim Morrison. .... is your name?
   It's Jane Street.

2 .... are you, Jane?
   I'm 22 years old, Mr Morrison.

3 .... were you born?
   In Bradford.

4 You're married, ... ?
   Yes, ...

5 .... do you live now?
   I live in Hampstead, with my husband.

6 You've got a job now, ... ?
   Yes, ...

7 .... do you want to leave?
   .... I want to earn more money, and work nearer my home.

8 .... long have you worked there?
   About three years.

9 .... do you do in your present job?
   I am a secretary and administrator.

10 .... do you start working in the morning?
    At 9 o'clock.

11 Right, and you finish at five, ... ?
    Yes, ... did you know?

12 Most companies do. .... did you start working?
    Four years ago. I was eighteen.

13 You've seen the description of this job, ... ?
    Yes, ...

14 Do you want to ask any questions about it?
    Yes, please. .... big is the company?
    It has two hundred employees.

15 You are the general manager, ... ?
    Yes, ...

16 The company hasn't been here long, ... ?
    No, ... It moved here from Manchester in 1990.

17 The company makes cars, ... ?
    Yes, ... But it also makes lorries.

18 .... lorries does it make?
    Only small lorries, up to three tons.

19 You won't want me to work overtime, ... ?
    No, ... But the hours are longer than you work now.

20 Oh. .... will I start in the mornings?
    At 8.30 am.

21 But I'll finish at 4.30, ... ?
    No, ... You'll finish at six.

22 But I have an hour for lunch, ... ?
    No, ... You only have half an hour.

23 That's nine hours a day! You haven't always worked those hours, ... ?
    No, ...

24 .... did you start doing that?
    When the recession started. You can't be lazy in a recession, ... ?
    No, I suppose(*sigh*) not.

AND   BUT   (linking clauses - 1)

Look at these pictures, and study the texts.

Fred is English.   He lives in Hampton.
- and -
Fred is English, and he lives in Hampton.

This is a good book.   Fred doesn't like it.
- but -
This is a good book, but Fred doesn't like it.

① Now complete these sentences with AND or BUT.

1   It was a very popular film, ... we enjoyed it.
2   It was a very popular film, ... we didn't enjoy it.
3   Robert is a good student, ... he always does his homework.
4   Carol is a good student, ... she never does her homework.

USE
A   We use **AND** when the second sentence *agrees* with the first sentence: Victoria went to Manchester, and Dennis went with her.
B   We use **BUT** when the second sentence *disagrees* with the first sentence: Victoria went to Liverpool, but Dennis didn't go.

FORM
We use **AND** to join words or sentences. We use **BUT** to join sentences. **Words:** Carol and Robert   knives and forks   "War and Peace" **Sentences:** Carol stayed. She talked to Robert. ➔ Carol stayed, and talked to Robert.   Carol stayed. She didn't talk to Tom ➔ Carol stayed, but she didn't talk to Tom.

True or False?

② Study the information, and read the sentences. Two of them are true and two are false.
Tick (✓) the true ones, and rewrite the false ones.

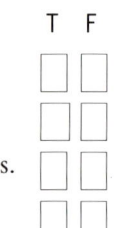

	Play golf	Like music
Robert	✓	✗
Carol	✗	✓

                                                                                    T   F
1   Carol likes music, but Robert doesn't.   ☐ ☐
2   Robert plays golf, and Carol does too.   ☐ ☐
3   Carol doesn't play golf, but Robert does.   ☐ ☐
4   Robert likes music, but Carol doesn't.   ☐ ☐

Some Facts About the Family

③ Complete each sentence three times, using AND or BUT.

1	Fred likes yogurt,	.... often eats it for breakfast.
		.... he never buys it.
		.... he takes one to school every day.

2	Robert is very healthy,	.... he never plays sport.
		.... he runs every morning.
		.... he doesn't smoke.

3	Dennis is a good driver,	.... he had an accident last week.
		.... he likes driving.
		.... his eyes are not very good.

And and But

④ Study this information,...

March:	Mabel booked three hotels for a driving holiday.
15th June:	Victor sold the old car.
1st-15th July:	Victor and Mabel went on holiday.
15th August:	Mabel bought a small new car.

... and now complete these sentences with AND or BUT.

1 Mabel booked a holiday for July, ... Victor was pleased.
2 She told Victor about the holiday, ... he forgot.
3 Victor sold the family car, ... he didn't buy a new one, ... he didn't tell Mabel.
4 They needed a car for the holiday, ... they didn't have one, ... Mabel was very annoyed with Victor.
5 Mabel had some money, ... she bought a small car.
6 Mabel chose the new car, ... Victor didn't like it!
7 They went on holiday, ... Mabel didn't let Victor drive!

⑤ Look at the picture, and complete these sentences with AND or BUT and a phrase.

Example: That's a desk lamp,........*but there is no*.................(bulb)

1 That's a coffee pot, ... (handle)
2 There's one chair .... (four legs)
3 That's a computer, ... (keyboard)
4 There's a desk, ... (three drawers)
5 There is the telephone, ... (wire)

BEFORE/AFTER SO AND BUT (linking clauses – 2)

Look at these pictures, and study the texts.

Robert's girlfriend Jenny is always late. Yesterday, they were going to the movies...

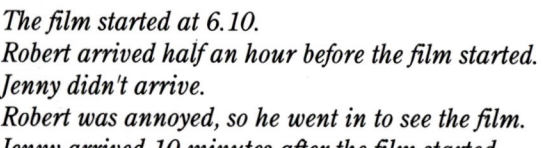

The film started at 6.10.
Robert arrived half an hour before the film started.
Jenny didn't arrive.
Robert was annoyed, so he went in to see the film.
Jenny arrived 10 minutes after the film started.

① Now complete these sentences with BEFORE, AFTER or SO.

1 She was tired, ... she went to bed.
2 She cleaned her teeth .... she went to bed.
3 She fell asleep 5 minutes .... she went to bed.
4 At 3 am she was cold, ... she put her bedsocks on.

USE
A We use **BEFORE** and **AFTER** to show time differences.
He had a shower before he had breakfast.
He had breakfast after he had a shower.
B We use **SO** when one action is the result of another.
It was raining, so she got wet.
He was tired, so he went to bed.

② Complete these, using AND, BUT and SO once in each sentence.

                                          .... she looked in a shoe shop.
1 Carol needed some new shoes, ... she didn't have any money.
                                          .... she wanted a coat.

                                          .... they occasionally bite people.
2 Dogs are loyal animals, ... they are used as guard dogs.
                                          .... children love them.

A Question of Timing

③ Read this passage!

> *Peter and Carol arranged to meet at 18.15. But Carol made a mistake; she thought 18.15 was*
> *8.15 pm! Peter was punctual, but he left the cafe at 7.30 pm. Carol arrived at the cafe at 8.15 pm.*

Now complete the story with words from the box.

and but so
before after

A   Peter left the cafe .... Carol arrived. *before*
after
Carol arrived .... Peter left.
Carol went to the cafe because she wanted to see Peter, ... he wasn't there, ... she *but* *so*
left .... went home. *and*

The story continues...

and but so

B   When Carol got home, the phone rang. Carol answered, ... it wasn't Peter. She waited *but*
for an hour, ... he didn't come, ... she went out again .... walked to the ice- *but* *so* *and*
cream parlour. He wasn't there either, ... she went home again .... found him *so* *and*
standing outside her house, waiting for her. It was 9 pm (21.00!); he smiled at her and they kissed.

Carol and Susan Are Going Together, But Where – and When?

Study this information.

Festival Theatre
HAMLET
by W Shakespeare
•
A new production
3 pm and 7.30 pm

(On Monday Carol bought the
tickets for the afternoon
performance.)

Society of Arts
IS PEACE POSSIBLE?
•
A lecture by S Genoves
Friday October 4th
4 pm

(On Tuesday the invitation
for the lecture arrived.)

Now complete these sentences with words from the box.

and but so
before after

1   The invitation to the lecture arrived .... Carol bought the tickets for the theatre.
2   Carol wanted to go to the theatre, ... Susan said the lecture was very good.
3   Susan won the argument, ... Carol changed the tickets to the evening performance.
4   They went to the lecture, and they had time for coffee .... they went to the theatre.
5   Carol was pleased, ... Susan was also pleased!

WHEN (time)

Look at the picture, and study the text.

"Will you see Sarah tomorrow at the office?"
"Yes, she is there every day."
"OK, can you give her this letter when you see her?"
"Sure, I'll give it to her when I see her."

① Now complete these sentences with a verb from the box and WILL or CAN, if necessary.

see	put
get	speak

1   "............. you .... to Fred when he gets home?"
2   "Yes, I'll speak to him when I .... him."
3   "Dennis, can you start cooking supper when you .... home?"
4   "All right. I .... the meat in the oven when I arrive."

USE
A   We use **WHEN**, like this:

	Will (etc.)	WHEN	*Present Tense*
	He will phone us	when	he arrives.
	He can phone us	when	he arrives.

	Imperative	WHEN	*Present Tense*
	Phone us	when	he arrives.

B   Word Order: He will phone us when he arrives.
                                When he arrives, he will phone us.

Good English?

② Look at the <u>underlined</u> parts of these sentences. Three of them are correct and three are wrong.
Tick (✓) the correct ones, and rewrite the wrong ones.

.............1 Tell me <u>when you are</u> ready.
.............2 You can go <u>when you will want</u> to.
.............3 I will leave <u>when the other girl arrives</u>.
.............4 He goes to bed <u>when he will be</u> tired.
.............5 Fasten your seat belts <u>when the sign will be</u> on.
.............6 Will you do it? Yes, I'll do it <u>when I can</u>.

Making a Cake

③ Match the two halves of each sentence.

1	When you make a cake, ...	A	don't open the oven door.
2	When you mix the ingredients, ...	B	serve it with tea or coffee.
3	When you put the milk in, ...	C	make sure you put in the correct amount.
4	When you put the cake in the oven, ...	D	take it out and put it on a plate.
5	When the cake is cooking, ...	E	first look at the instructions.
6	When the cake is ready, ...	F	check that the oven is hot.
7	When you give the cake to your guests, ...	G	put it in slowly and stir the mixture.

④ Now complete these sentences with WHEN and the correct form of a verb from the box.

> come   turn   begin
> post   see

1   Have you posted that letter yet?
    No, I've nearly finished it. .... I finish it, I .... it.
2   What time will you be here? About six.
    Right. I .... you .... you arrive.
3   Has Sue arrived yet?
    No. I'll leave .... she ....
4   He was making tea .... the earthquake ....
5   The bus moved forward .... the traffic light .... green.

Have you got a child? Children grow and change, and they do and want different things.

⑤ Complete these sentences in a similar way to number one. (The exact age is not important.)

1   When he's six months old, he'll start to crawl.
2   .... , he'll start to walk.
3   .... , he'll start to speak.
4   .... , he won't want to stay in his playpen.
5   .... , he'll start primary school.

⑥ Complete these sentences with a phrase from the box.

> he'll go to university.   he'll have his own flat.
> he'll want to drive your car.   he'll start shaving.

1   When he's about 14, ...
2   When he's about 16, ...
3   When he's about 18, ...
4   When he's about 21, ...

IF (condition)

Look at the picture, and study the text.

"Will you see Tim tomorrow at the office?"
"I don't know; he's not there every day."
"Oh, well, can you give him this letter if you see him?"
"Yes, I'll give it to him if I see him."

① Now complete these sentences with a verb from the box, in future, present or imperative.

> be   catch
> die   break

1   .... the baby if you see she is falling.
2   Fred runs away if he .... a window.
3   The fish .... if the water in the fishbowl dries up.
4   If he .... late again, I shall be furious!

USE

Condition
We use **IF**, like this:

***Will* (etc.)**	IF	***Present Tense***
He will tell him	if	he sees him.
He can tell him	if	he sees him.

Present Tense	IF	***Present Tense***
You get wet	if	it rains.

Imperative	IF	***Present Tense***
Phone me	if	you like.

Good English?

② Look at the <u>underlined</u> parts of these sentences. Eight of them are correct and four are wrong. Tick (✓) the correct ones, and rewrite the wrong ones.

.... 1   <u>Come</u> for tea if you <u>have</u> time.
.... 2   She <u>will understand</u> if you <u>will explain</u> the problem.
.... 3   I <u>come</u> tomorrow if the weather <u>is</u> good.
.... 4   We <u>will cancel</u> the game if it <u>rains</u>.
.... 5   I <u>buy</u> it if I <u>will have</u> the money.
.... 6   If it'<u>s</u> not too late, we'<u>ll have</u> supper after the theatre.

③ Complete each sentence with an appropriate form of a verb from the box.

> go   feel
> lose   get

1   If you .... your passport, go to the Embassy and tell them.
2   She .... very upset if I lose this beautiful bracelet.
3   If you go to the cinema early you .... a seat.
4   We .... to the beach if the weather is nice.

> be   take
> lend   telephone

5   If you witness a crime, ... the police.
6   I will go to bed if I .... sleepy.
7   "If you .... your umbrella, you won't get wet."
8   I .... you my bicycle if you need it.

④ Now complete these sentences with IF and the correct form of a verb from the box.

> take   find

1   "Did I leave my wallet in your house?"
    "I haven't seen it. But .... I .... it , I'll give it to you."
2   "Look at the time!"
    "............. you .... (not) .... a taxi, you'll be late!"

⑤ Make up sentences in the same way as the example.

Example: *Condition*   *Consequence*
           you go to bed late   you get up late
    If you go to bed late, you'll get up late.

Condition	*Consequence*
1 you get up late	you miss your train
2 you miss your train	you're late to the office
3 you're late to the office	your boss is angry
4 your boss is angry	you lose your job (possibly)
5 you lose your job	your wife leaves you
6 your wife leaves you	you are very unhappy

Conclusion: Don't go to bed late!

THE MAN WHO KNEW TOO MUCH
THE MOUSE THAT ROARED   (relative clauses – 1)

Look at these pictures, and study the texts.

*This is the man
who knew too much.*

*This is the gun
that was used for the murder.*

① Now complete these sentences, using WHO or THAT.

1   Carol was the woman .... came to dinner.
2   I can't find the milk .... was in the fridge.
3   Robert works for the a company .... sells tractors.
4   Jim is the person .... sold his old car.

USE

A   **WHO** is for people:
      This is the man. The man knew too much.
      This is the man who knew too much.

      The woman – the woman came to dinner – was very nice.
      The woman who came to dinner was very nice.

B   **THAT** is for things and animals:
      This is the company. The company makes cars.
      This is the company that makes cars.

Note: We sometimes use THAT for people (but not WHO for things and animals):
      THAT   Things, animals and sometimes people
      WHO   People only

Good English?

② Look at the <u>underlined</u> parts of these sentences. Three of them are correct and three are wrong.
Tick (✓) the correct ones and rewrite the wrong ones.

.............1 This is <u>the boy who he is going</u> to join the class.
.............2 Fred plays in a football <u>team that always loses</u>!
.............3 <u>The girl answered the phone</u> said Mr Smith was out.
.............4 The Curies were <u>the couple who discovered radium</u>.
.............5 Is that <u>the car that always breaks down</u>?
.............6 A dictionary is <u>a book who defines</u> words.

What Do These People Do?

③ Now you have to complete these sentences, using WHO and a suitable sentence from the box.

Tip: Don't forget to omit something from each sentence in the box!

> He or she drives a taxi.   He or she teaches in a school.
> He or she repairs cars.   He or she looks after patients.
> He or she works in a restaurant.

1   A doctor is a person ....
2   A teacher is someone ....
3   A waiter is a person ....
4   A mechanic is someone ....
5   A driver is a person ....

What Do These Organisations Do?

④ Here are some more sentences to complete, this time using THAT and a suitable sentence from the box.

> It protects the environment.   It makes cars.
> It makes television sets.   It started the Common Market.
> It lends money to developing countries.

1   Sony is a Japanese company ....
2   Greenpeace is an association ....
3   The Treaty of Rome was the treaty ....
4   The World Bank is an organisation ....
5   Ford is an American company ....

The Diamond Robbery

⑤ You have to complete the sentences below, using the information from the pictures.

"This man stole the diamond."

"This hammer was used to break the glass."

"This diamond was stolen."

"This guard caught the criminal."

"This woman phoned the police."

"These keys were used to open the museum doors."

1   You can see the man ....
2   You can see the hammer ....
3   You can see the diamond ....
4   You can see the guard ....
5   You can see the woman ....
6   You can see the keys ....

THE WOMAN HE SAW (relative clauses – 2)

Look at these pictures, and study the texts.

That was the woman he saw.

*He was the man
who knew too much!*

That's the house he's building.

*He's using bricks
that fall off lorries!*

① Now complete these sentences with WHO, THAT or NOTHING (-).

1 There is the house .... he lived in.
2 That is the man .... saw us.
3 This is the motorcycle .... caused the accident.
4 There is the man .... we saw.
5 This is the car .... broke the speed record.

FORM
A **WHO** That is the man. The man saw us.   That is the man who saw us.
B **(WHO)** That is the man. We saw the man.   That is the man (–) we saw.
C **THAT** That is the car. The car broke the record.   That is the car that broke the record.
D **(THAT)** That is the car. I drove the car.   That is the car (–) I drove.
Note: In numbers B and D, we do not have to use WHO and THAT.

② Look at the <u>underlined</u> parts of these sentences. Two of them are correct and two are wrong.
   Tick (✔) the correct ones, and rewrite the wrong ones.

.... 1 This is <u>the coat who I bought it</u> yesterday.
.... 2 There is <u>the man who came</u> to see me.
.... 3 <u>The girls came</u> to supper were from Brazil.
.... 4 Where is <u>the newspaper I brought</u> home?

More Practice

③ You have to complete each sentence with WHO, THAT or NOTHING (-).

    1   The food .... I ate yesterday was awful.
    2   The person .... cooked the food was a terrible cook.
    3   The potatoes .... they gave me were as hard as rocks.
    4   The sauce .... goes with the meat was cold.
    5   And the waiter .... I spoke to was rude!

Completions Without WHO or THAT

④ Complete each sentence with a sentence from the box. Omit the part in *italics* in this exercise and the next. *Tip*: Don't forget to omit part of the sentence in the boxes.

We use *the room* for lectures.	You talked to *the teacher* this morning.
You'll see *the students* every day.	We can use *the photocopier*.
We all use *the cafeteria*.	We are studying *the book* this month.

Example: ......*Here is the room we use for lectures.*.....................

    1   Look, there's the teacher ....
    2   This is the book ....
    3   Here is the cafeteria ....
    4   There are the students ....
    5   And here is the photocopier ....

WHO, THAT or Nothing (–)

⑤ Complete each sentence using a sentence from the box for each one. Use WHO, THAT or nothing (-).

The butter was in the fridge.	The girl got the job.
Tom recommended the hotel.	I saw the boy hiding behind the sofa.

    1   Dennis and Victoria spent a week at the hotel ....
    2   The girl .... was Carol.
    3   I can't find the butter ....
    4   The boy .... was Fred - of course!

Fred kicked the ball.	(x2) Auntie Mabel was sitting with a man.
The window was broken.	I saw Carol.

    5   Carol is the girl .... walking to the university.
    6   That's the window .... in the football game.
    7   That's the ball ....
    8   The woman .... is Auntie Mabel.
    9   The man .... is her husband, Uncle Victor.

MIXED EXERCISES (units 75 - 80)

Here are two stories which use all the words practised in Units 75 - 80 (except AND).

but	before	when	that
so	after	who	(that)
because	if	(who)	

The First Story: Susan's Adventure With the Burglar

① Read this story and fill in the blanks. Think about each blank and put in the best word from the ones listed above in the box. Sometimes there are two possible answers – but don't use AND.

1 My name is Susan, and I live with my husband Raymond. I want to tell you about something .... happened to us yesterday.

2 I usually wake up about 7 am, ... yesterday I woke up at 6.45 am .... I heard a noise.

3 At first I thought I was dreaming, ... I heard the noise again, ... I woke my husband.

4 "What's the matter?" he said .... he woke up. "I heard a noise .... woke me up," I said.

5 .... a few seconds I heard it again. "That's a man .... is walking about downstairs," I said. "............. I hear it again, I'll call the police."

6 I heard the noise again, ... I picked up the telephone and dialled 999.

7 A voice said, "Police, Fire or Ambulance?" "Police!" I said, "............. be quick!" .... a few moments a voice said, "Police."

8 "Come quickly .... there's a man downstairs!" I said.

9 The police were very quick, and .... we got dressed, they arrived. The policemen found the front door open, ... they came in to the house, ... they didn't catch the intruder. He left .... they arrived.

10 .... we heard the police, we both went downstairs in our dressing gowns, ... there wasn't time to dress.

11 "Did you see the man .... broke in?" they asked us. "No, we didn't see him," I said, "............. I heard him .... he opened the door."

12 "The man .... you heard is an expert," said the sergeant, "............. he opened the front door easily. The lock .... you have got is a good one, ... he opened it anyway."

13 "............. you want to sleep easily, buy a new lock," said one of the policemen. "The man .... opened this door will probably come back."

14 "We thought the lock .... we had was a good one," my husband said. "We'll have to buy a lock .... is even better."

15 "Would you like a cup of tea .... you go?" I said to the policemen. "No thank you, ma'am, we can't stop .... we're on duty," they said, and they left.

The Second Story: A Second Honeymoon

② Now read this story and fill in the blanks. Again, think about each blank, and put in the best word from the ones listed on the previous page. Sometimes there are two possible answers – but don't use AND.

1   Twenty years ago, Walter and Mary got married, ... they didn't have any money ....
    they stayed at home for their honeymoon. They were happy anyway .... they liked to be
    together.

2   .... they were married for five years, they started to go on holiday every year. The hotels
    .... they stayed in were not very good, ... they didn't mind.

3   Last year, they went to see their travel agents .... they wanted to go to Greece on March
    15th, ... the plane to Athens was full on that day, ... they changed to March 17th.

4   On March 17th they arrived at the airport two hours .... the plane was due to leave. The
    airline .... they were using was called Air England.

5   .... they got on the plane, they went through Immigration. The Immigration Officer
    .... saw them was very friendly.

6   .... they landed in Athens, they took a taxi to the hotel .... they had booked.

7   .... they went to the room, they saw it was a single room, ... they went downstairs
    and asked for a double.

8   The desk clerk said, "You can have a double room .... you pay double." Walter was
    angry, and said, "............. we booked this holiday in London, we said we wanted a double
    room .... there are two of us."

9   "Well, the person .... booked you made a mistake," said the desk clerk. "There's nothing
    .... I can do about it."

10 "............. you don't give us a double room I shall complain to the manager!" said Walter,
    .... was very angry.

11 "The only double room .... is empty is the honeymoon suite. You can have that,
    .... it costs $200 a night."

12 "I don't want a honeymoon suite .... I've been married for 20 years!" shouted Walter.

13 A man .... was standing next to them said quietly, "I always take my wife to a
    honeymoon suite .... I can afford it."

14 Walter looked at his wife, ... was smiling, and he said to the desk clerk, "All right,
    .... that's the only room .... you've got, we'll take it."

15 .... twenty years of marriage, Walter and Mary had a honeymoon suite!

IT IS   THEY ARE   THERE IS   THERE ARE

Look at these pictures, and study the texts.

What is it?
It's a bowl of soup,
but there's a fly in it!

What are they?
They are sheep, but there are
some black sheep too!

① Complete these sentences with IT, THEY or THERE.

1   .... are some flower pots on the table.

2   .... 're not flower pots, ... 're vases.

3   And .... 's a handbag on the chair.

4   .... is not a handbag, ... 's a briefcase.

USE

A   We use **IT IS/THEY ARE** for definition
(when you want to say what something is):
          What is it? It's a mosquito.
          What are those things? They are flower pots.

B   We use **THERE IS** for existence
(when you want to say that something exists, or is present):
          There's an insect on your neck.
          There are five assistant managers in the company.
          There were five assistant managers in my last company.

FORM

	IT		**THERE**	
	Present	*Past*	*Present*	*Past*
Singular	It is	It was	There is	There was
Plural	They are	They were	There are	There were

Good English?

② Look at the <u>underlined</u> parts of these sentences. Three of them are correct and four are wrong.
Tick (✓) the correct ones, and rewrite the wrong ones.

.... 1   <u>They are</u> 27 rooms in the palace.

.... 2   Inside the palace, <u>there are</u> a lot of pictures.

.... 3   <u>They are</u> all Spanish and Italian pictures.

.... 4   Outside, <u>it is</u> a lovely garden, with a lake.

.... 5   <u>Is</u> a small lake.

.... 6   What are those big birds? <u>There are</u> swans.

.... 7   <u>It is</u> a beautiful palace.

More Practice

③ Complete these sentences with IT, THEY or THERE, and an appropriate form of the verb BE.

1   The Johnsons live in an old house. Years before, *it was* Mr Johnson's father's house.
2   .... a big house.
3   .... happy living together.
4   .... three animals in the house: Winston, Sally and the fish.
5   .... four animals last year, but one of the fish died.
6   .... all very sad, because they were fond of the fish.

④ Rewrite these sentences, beginning with THERE IS/ARE WAS/WERE.

Example: Fifty people were at the lecture.
        There were fifty people at the lecture.

1   Six men were in the room. ....
2   We have a meeting every Monday. ....
3   A man is waiting for you. ....
4   Two lions are in the big cage. ....
5   Some books were on the table. Where are they now? ....
6   The interval was long – nearly half an hour! ....
7   An old woman was standing outside my house. ....
8   Three students are standing outside your office, Mr Smith. ....
9   We heard a loud explosion and the light went out. ....
10 Plenty of people were at the party. ....

It's a Mad, Mad (Dangerous!) World!

⑤ Complete these sentences with IT, THEY or THERE.

1   .... is something on my collar!
    Is .... a spider?

2   .... isn't a spider;
    .... 's a cockroach!

3   Help! .... 're very dirty animals!

4   Don't worry, ... aren't dangerous.

5   Yes .... are; they carry diseases!

6   Don't worry about the cockroach; .... 's a snake crawling about on your left foot!

7   Oh my goodness! Is .... a poisonous snake?

8   I don't know. But .... are two scorpions on your leg.
    .... 're poisonous, I'm sure.

9   Aaaaaaah!!! Well, don't just stand there; do something before .... bite me!
    I can't; ....'s a lion coming towards me, and ....'s got big teeth!
    Goodbye!

WORD ORDER (adjectives and prepositions)

Word order in English is important. Look at these pictures, and answer the question.

Which is which?   *THE DOG IS BITING THE MAN.*
          THE MAN IS BITING THE DOG.

Now study these texts.

> *The dog is biting the man.*
> *He is ready.*   *Is he ready?*
> *This is a book.*   *What is this?*

① Now you have to put these words in the right order to make good sentences. (Don't forget punctuation and capital letters!)

    1   is/a tree/it ....
    2   is/a tree/it/.. ?
    3   not/right/is/Brian ....
    4   eating/woman/lunch/is/her/the ....
    5   raining/is/it ....
    6   those/apples/are .... ?
    7   was/there/he/not ....
    8   they/English/were ....
    9   French/is/she ....
    10   home/boy/ball/the/the/took ....
    11   right/I/am .... ?
    12   bad/not/that/is ....

Now study these phrases, and notice the position of the adjectives.

> *... the red book*   *... the big bottle*
> *... the French cook*   *... an interesting stor.*
> *... a very good joke*

② Now you have to put these in order.

    1   likes/teacher/the/he/German ....
    2   baby/is/she/beautiful/a ....
    3   nice/they/have/a/house ....
    4   very/is/old/that/a/coat ....
    5   she/new/buying/is/curtains ....
    6   book/difficult/was/a/that ....
    7   woman/clever/she/very/is/a ....

Statement and Request

③ Now you have to put these sentences in order.

1 left/have/they/not ....
2 not/John/go/did ....
3 she/is/today/leaving .... ?
4 the/time/you/do/know .... ?
5 finished/have/they .... ?
6 lunch/are/they/having/not ....
7 him/do/not/like/I ....
8 goodbye/say/she/did .... ?
9 that/do/he/not/can ....
10 he/not/wait/must ....

WH- Questions

Now study these questions with words like WHEN etc.

When is she going to Florence?
Who is she going with?

④ Now you have to put these WH- questions in order.

1 gone/where/John/has .... ?
2 next/leave/when/train/the/does .... ?
3 her/you/time/expecting/what/are .... ?
4 late/Victoria/home/did/why/get .... ?
5 John/with/is/who/working .... ?
6 month/getting/how/on/this/you/are .... ?
7 arrive/train/next/does/when/the .... ?
8 Carol/to/what/say/Robert/did .... ?
9 Fred/waiting/why/for/we/are..................... ?
10 everybody/where/to/has/gone .... ?

English From Another Planet!

⑤ These expressions are in the English spoken on another planet. Can you change the order to the order used on this planet?

Strong you are, and clever.
Strong in you the Force is.
The power of the Empire,
great it is and wicked.
(with apologies to the makers of "Star Wars!")

CAPITAL LETTERS and PUNCTUATION

Capital Letters

Look at these examples.

Uncle Victor once visited Entebbe in Uganda.
We bought our Christmas cards at the newsagents.
"What's the time?" asked Mrs Williams.
I saw him in the autumn, in September or October.
Victoria likes Italian shoes.

Carol loves Hungarian food.
Robert speaks a little German.
I'm waiting for Professor Watson.
It's Wednesday, the 14th of March.
Janet Wilson is English.

USE
We use CAPITAL LETTERS with these words:

We use CAPITAL LETTERS with these words:
1. The first letter of a sentence:
    They came home. The concert was good.
2. Names of people, and their titles:
    Susan John Smith Dr Jones Mrs Samuels
3. Names of towns, countries, languages, nationalities:
    London New York Great Britain English French
4. Days and Months (but not seasons):
    Monday Wednesday Friday January April September
    (But: spring summer autumn winter)
5. Names of shops, companies etc:
    Harrods Woolworths Chrysler Sony Colgate
    Imperial Chemical Industries (ICI)
6. Titles of books, newspapers, magazines:
    War and Peace The Daily Mail "Computer World"
7. Street, road, avenue etc., if it part of the name:
    Oxford Street Camden Road
8. The names of famous buildings and places:
    Buckingham Palace The Louvre
9. The word "I"

Good English?

① There are nine mistakes in these sentences. Underline the mistakes and correct them.

1 John and mary got up late on tuesday.

....

2 they went to a big Shop in Smith Street and bought a shirt.

....

3 In May they went to paris, and in the Autumn they went to London.

....

4 they learned american english when they lived in California.

....

Punctuation

② Look at these punctuation marks. What are their names? Put the correct letter under each one. (One has been done for you.)

?   !   '   " "   .   :   ;   ,

....d..   ....

a	exclamation mark	d	colon	g	apostrophe
b	quotation marks	e	semicolon	h	comma
c	full stop (USA: period)	f	question mark		

Punctuation: Questions, Exclamations, Apostrophes and Quotations

Look at these examples.

What are you doing, John?   *Peter's shirt isn't dry.*

That's terrible! What a mess! Help!   *"Good Morning," he said politely.*

③ Rewrite these sentences with capital letters, question marks, exclamation marks, apostrophes and quotation marks (and full stops at the end if necessary).

1   hes a really wonderful man

....

2   im afraid he doesnt know what hes doing

....

3   do you know what the time is he asked

....

4   they live in madrid so they speak spanish quite well

....

5   whats the quickest way to the railway station

....

6   youve made a terrible mess

....

7   fred hasnt done his french homework

....

8   can you hear me he said

....

9   they cant tell you because theyre strangers here

....

10   robert goes to work by car from monday to friday in the winter but from april to august he usually cycles

....

11   she wants to be a correspondent for the new york times

....

12   have you read king lear by shakespeare she asked me

....

13   help im drowning

....

14   our two children susan and peter were born in dublin

....

15   wheres john he asked me

....

PUNCTUATION

Full Stops and Capitals

Read these sentences, and notice the full stops and capital letters.

Robert lives in Hampton. He travels to work every day.

① Now rewrite the following, inserting one or two full stops (and capital letters where necessary!) in each one.

1   fred is a nice lad he lives with his parents

....

2   robert met an old school friend they talked all night

....

3   uncle victor and auntie mabel are married they have been together for 40 years

....

4   I was late home last night about 6 o'clock and an old friend phoned me at the office he was in trouble and wanted to talk

....

Commas

Read these sentences, and notice the commas.

He brought bread, a carton of milk, some jam and a cake.
I waited for an hour, but he didn't come.
Robert, the tall young man over there, is Carol's elder brother.
I left at six o'clock, and John left an hour later.

② Now rewrite the following, inserting one or two commas in each one.

1   "Carol the girl with blonde hair is my sister."

....

2   He asked his bank for a loan but the answer was no.

....

3   "You'll need some sweaters a warm coat a hat and a scarf."

....

4   Victoria got home in time for supper and Dennis arrived a few minutes later.

....

5   Peter Jones the man I told you about is coming tomorrow.

....

6   He bought a book some paper a pen and a pencil.

....

Semicolon

Read this sentence, and notice the semicolon.

Robert is very nice; I like him very much.

③ Now rewrite the following, inserting one semicolon in each one.

1   There aren't any envelopes I must go and buy some.

....

2   Here are the pencils you wanted I couldn't find any pens.

....

3   She's a very nice person let's invite her to supper.

....

4   I don't know what my husband wants I'll ask him tonight.

....

Colon

Read these sentences, and notice the colons.

Carol bought these items: a pizza, two cakes, and a lemonade.
Carol knew the answer: it was forty-two.

④ Now rewrite the following, inserting one colon in each one.

1   Robert told us a secret he wants to get married!

....

2   This is what Victoria packed for their day out sandwiches, a thermos of coffee and some biscuits.

....

3   This is what I want you to do go home and change your clothes and wait.

....

4   They had important news the war had ended.

....

Mixed Bag

⑤ Now rewrite the following, inserting full stops, commas, capitals, semicolons and colons. (There will be different opinions, and sometimes more than one good solution!)

1   john and mary came to see us last night they stayed for an hour but then left we were quite surprised we thought they would stay for dinner

....

....

2   carol stayed at home to do the cooking and robert went to the supermarket he bought a lot of things some tomatoes a few potatoes some meat a chicken and two bottles of wine

....

....

3   when I got up this morning I had a headache so I didn't go to the office about ten o'clock I phoned and told the boss I wasn't well he told me to stay at home

....

....

Here are the main tenses of the English verb, with FORM and USE:

1	The present simple	She works
2	The past simple	She worked
3	The present continuous (progressive)	She is working
4	The past continuous (progressive)	She was working
5	The present perfect	She has worked
6	The future: will	She will work
	present future	She is working
	going to	She is going to work
7	The passive: present	It is made
8	The passive: past	It was made

1   The Present Simple

FORM

	Singular	Plural
1st person	I walk	We walk
2nd person	You walk	You walk
3rd person	He	
	She walks	They walk
	It	

Different ways of adding "s" to 3rd person singular:

walk + s walks   buy + s buys

catch + es catches   try –y + ies tries

Forming negative and interrogative:

Negative

	Singular	Plural
1st person	I do not walk	We do not walk
2nd person	You do not walk	You do not walk
3rd person	He }	
	She } does not walk	They do not walk
	It }	

Interrogative

	Singular	Plural
1st person	Do I walk?	Do we walk?
2nd person	Do you walk?	Do you walk?
3rd person	Does { he / she / it } walk?	Do they walk?

For contractions, see Appendix 2

USE

1   Permanent or regular events:

They live here.

She plays tennis every Saturday.

2   'Eternal' truths:

Water boils at 100 °C.

2   The Past Simple

FORM

	Singular	*Plural*
1st person	I walked	We walked
2nd person	You walked	You walked
3rd person	He She It } walked	They walked.

Forming negative and interrogative:

Negative

	Singular	*Plural*
1st person	I did not walk	We did not walk
2nd person	You did not walk	You did not walk
3rd person	He She It } did not walk	They did not walk

Interrogative

	Singular	*Plural*
1st person	Did I walk?	Did we walk?
2nd person	Did you walk?	Did you walk?
3rd person	Did { he she it } walk?	Did they walk?

For contractions, see Appendix 2

USE

1   Events that started and finished in the past:
   The boy jumped off the bus.
   Columbus discovered America in 1492.
2   Past tense verbs often have an adverb of time:
   last year, 50 years ago, then, yesterday, etc.

3   The Present Continuous or Progressive

FORM

	Singular	*Plural*
1st person	I am walking	We are walking
2nd person	You are walking	You are walking
3rd person	He She It } is walking	They are walking

USE

1   Immediate present (happening now):
   You are reading this page now.
2   Temporary events, not necessarily happening now,
   but with a clear time limit on them:
   Jane is studying Polish these days.

Forming negative and interrogative:

Negative   I am not walking   She is not walking, etc.
Interrogative   Am I walking?   Is he walking? etc.

4   The Past Continuous or Progressive

FORM

	Singular	*Plural*
1st person	I was walking	We were walking
2nd person	You were walking	You were walking
3rd person	He ⎫ She ⎬ was walking They were walking It ⎭	

Forming negative and interrogative:

Negative   I was not walking   She was not walking, etc.
Interrogative   Was I walking?   Was he walking? etc.

USE

1   Interrupted events in the past:
      I was having supper when the phone rang.
2   Incomplete events:
      I was reading this book last night. (I didn't finish)

5   The Present Perfect

FORM

	Singular	*Plural*
1st person	I have walked	We have walked
2nd person	You have walked	You have walked
3rd person	He ⎫ She ⎬ has walked They have walked It ⎭	

Forming negative and interrogative:

Negative   I have not walked   She has not walked, etc.
Interrogative   Have I walked?   Has he walked? etc.

USE

1   An activity which starts in the past and continues to the present:
      I have lived here for 7 years.
2   This tense is often accompanied by:
      ... for 3 days
      ... since last Monday

It is not accompanied by a time adverb (yesterday, etc.).

6 The Future

FORM

1	WILL	I (etc.) will go
		I (etc.) will not go
		Will I (etc.) go?
2	-ING	(Same as present continuous: see above)
3	GOING TO	It is going to rain. Is it going to rain? It is not going to rain.

But Note: We often use the three different future forms indiscriminately, so students should not spend much time worrying about which one to use. People will usually understand any of the three.

USE

1	WILL	Especially for predictions, expressing certainty:
		It will snow in Moscow in December.
2	-ING	Especially for plans and programmes:
		The orchestra is playing Beethoven tonight.
		I am leaving at 6.15 tomorrow morning.
3	GOING TO	Especially for intentions:
		I'm going to be an engineer when I grow up.

7 Present Passive

FORM

	Singular	Plural
1st person	I was born	We were born
2nd person	You were born	You were born
3rd person	He } She } was born It }	They were born

Forming negative and interrogative:

Negative	I was not born	She was not born, etc.
Interrogative	Was I born?	Was he born? etc

USE

See below, past passive

8 The Past Passive

FORM

As for present passive, with past tense forms of the verb BE.

USE

We use the passive   when a) the grammatical subject is not important,
and   b) we want to emphasise something else, e.g. the time or the place or the grammatical object:
Examples:
The Berlin Wall was knocked down in 1989.
(This car was) made in Germany.

FORM

These words are contracted:

am	➔	*'m*		*I'm*
are	➔	*'re*		*They're*
is	➔	*'s*★	}	*She's*
has	➔	*'s*★		*He's*
have	➔	*'ve*		*I've*
will	➔	*'ll*		*We'll*
not	➔	*n't or 't*		*He isn't I can't*
will not	➔	*won't*		*I won't*

★ *'s* is a contraction for:

1 is: It's a boy!
2 has: He's gone.
3 Possessive: the girl's coat

When words are contracted, they are joined to the word before them:

I am ➔ I'm   they are ➔ they're

he is ➔ he's   they have ➔ they've

he is not ➔ he isn't   we can not ➔ we can't

The word the contraction is written with is usually a pronoun, but is sometimes a noun:

He's coming.

Peter's coming.

USE

1   **We use contractions** in speech (or writing which is like speech).

In speech, people nearly always use contractions (but see 2 below):

Hello, Mr Smith, how's your wife?

She's fine, thank you.

In writing, **we use contractions** if we want to be friendly, informal, or make sentences seem to be a conversation. You often see contractions in private letters, in newspapers, interviews etc:

Dear Sue,

I'm staying with friends …

2   **We do not use contractions** in writing (or speech which is like writing).

In writing, we don't usually use contractions, especially if the writing is formal, like a legal document or business letter, a serious article in a journal, etc. (but see above).

In speech, we don't use contractions if we want to be very formal:

"I have not had the opportunity to thank you all …"

or very emphatic:

"You must understand, I DID NOT DO IT!"

APPENDIX 3
IRREGULAR VERBS

Here is a list of the 39 irregular verbs in this book:

begin	began	begun	*pay*	pay	paid
buy	bought	bought	*put*	put	put
come	came	come	*read*	read	read
cost	cost	cost	*run*	ran	run
do	did	done	*say*	said	said
drink	drank	drunk	*see*	saw	seen
drive	drove	driven	*sell*	sold	sold
eat	ate	eaten	*sit*	sat	sat
get	got	got	*sleep*	slept	slept
give	gave	give	*speak*	spoke	spoken
go	went	gone	*spend*	spent	spent
have	had	had	*stand*	stood	stood
hear	heard	heard	*take*	took	taken
know	knew	known	*teach*	taught	taught
learn	learnt	learnt	*tell*	told	told
	(learned)	(learned)	*think*	thought	thought
leave	left	left	*understand*	–stood	–stood
make	made	made	*wake*	woke	waken
mean	meant	meant	*wear*	wore	worn
meet	met	met	*write*	wrote	written

The same verbs, divided into easy-to-remember groups:

1	"Almost regular" *Example*: heard, heard, heard	*have hear learn make pay say send*
2	"No change" *Example*: put, put, put	*cost put*
3	"The vowel changes" *Example*: get, got, got	*get meet read sit*
4	"The vowel changes + 't'" *Example:* leave, left, left	*leave sleep mean*
5	"The vowel changes + 'd'" *Example*: sell, sold, sold	*sell tell stand understand*
6	"-ght" *Example*: buy, bought, bought	*buy teach think*
7	"The vowel changes twice: to 'a' and to 'u'" *Example*: begin, began, begun	*begin come drink run*
8	"The vowel changes twice, and you add 'en' or 'n'" *Example*: drive, drove, driven	*drive eat give know speak see take wake wear write*
9	"Everything changes!"	*go be*